SOURCE BOOKS ON EDUCATION

THE EDUCATION OF WOMEN IN THE UNITED STATES
A Guide to Theory, Teaching, and Research

Averil Evans McClelland

GARLAND PUBLISHING, INC. • NEW YORK & LONDON
1992

Library of Congress Cataloging-in-Publication Data

McClelland, Averil.
  The education of women in the United States : a guide to theory,
teaching, and research / by Averil Evans McClelland.
      p.   cm. — (Garland reference library of social science ; vol.
551. Source books on education ; vol. 23.)
  Includes index.
  ISBN 0-8240-4842-3 (alk. paper)
      1. Women—Education—United States. 2. Women—Education—
United States—Bibliography.   I. Title. II. Series: Garland reference
library of social science ; vol. 551. III. Series: Garland reference
library of social science. Source books on education ; vol. 23.
LC1752.M34   1992
376'.973—dc20   91-14495
                                                                          CIP

Printed on acid-free, 250-year-life paper
Manufactured in the United States of America

DEDICATION

For my mother, Florence Evans, and my aunts, Eleanor Laforney and Frances Whittington, who are the educated women who preceded me; and for my daughter, Megan McClelland Kaplar, and my nieces, Lauren McClelland, Heather Cross, and Erin Cross, who carry the hopes of educated women into the next generation.

TABLE OF CONTENTS

Contents ix

INDICES

PREFACE

The bibliography presented in this book introduces the reader to the general subject of the education of girls and women in the United States, with some reference to historical antecedents in western civilization beginning with the ancient Greeks. It is offered as a guide to further research on the subject, which is badly needed, and is intended for use primarily by scholars in education and other social sciences, scholars in women's studies, classroom teachers, and any in the general public who are interested in the consequences of gender for females in schools and other educational settings.

The subject of the education of women is defined broadly, in terms of major themes which weave together the diverse elements of women's educational experiences. The bibliography is selective for a number of reasons. First, since the audience for this work includes teachers and interested members of the public who may not have ready access to some of the more specialized references, one criterion of selection is the availability of the sources. For this reason, a great variety of primary material contained in letters, diaries, journals, and other personal writing, as well as contemporary biographies and autobiographies which are often found in special collections housed in university and college libraries and local museums has been omitted. In general, items in the bibliography include books, journal articles, essay and other reviews, chapters and essays in collected works, dissertations and some other unpublished work. It is believed that all of these can be found in or through public library systems if college and university libraries are not easily available.

Second, the bibliography is selective because it is intended to represent the *literature* on women's education, which is also selective. There is considerable work, for example, on the development of higher education for middle-class women, but not a great deal on the education of lower-class working women. Similarly, there is a great deal of work on white women, and much less on women of color. In some cases, as will be obvious, work on education still lies embedded in more general work on the life experience of particular groups of women. Because this is the case, and because much literature on women's education is contained in survey articles and books which cover a number of time periods, not all items in the bibliography can be placed in each section to which they may refer. For this reason, bibliographic entries are numbered consecutively and referred to in the text by that number wherever they are cited.

Third, as might be expected, only material in English has been selected for presentation. This decision limits much of the bibliography to secondary sources in the section on European education, but was made because many of the primary sources from non-English speaking countries have not been translated. However, an attempt has been made to include primary sources which contain major plans for the education of women written by both men and women.

Because of the selectivity of the bibliography, care has been taken throughout to include entries which in themselves contain ample references to primary sources for the reader who is interested in and able to pursue more specialized inquiry.

Bibliographical material is organized first by theme and second by chronology. The book is divided into three major parts and eight chapters. Part I discusses some issues in researching women's educational history as well as suggesting some historical themes in female education from early Greece to the eighteenth century in Europe and from the seventeenth century to contemporary times in the United States. Part II addresses the varied purposes for which girls and women were educated in the United States: housewifery, motherhood, paid work, civic responsibility, and intellectual endeavors. Part III examines some contemporary issues of gender and education in schooling, educational leadership, higher education, educational reform, and the education of teachers. Each of the three parts and each chapter is introduced with an essay, and relevant bibliographic entries are listed at the end of each chapter.

The research method used for this survey is a fairly simple one. Two initial searches were made, one through the ERIC database and one in major education and women's studies journals from 1970 to the present. This information was cross-checked for duplication, and then a large sample of the citations was obtained, read, and culled for further sources. When using this method, two consequences are readily apparent. First, one can be fairly certain that major works in the field will be discovered through repeated citation. Second, references within bibliographic sources point to an incredible richness of material for further inquiry—a richness which is both tantalizing and frustrating. Limitations of both time and space require that even the most provocative lines of inquiry—for example, the precise ways in which a long list of "feminine virtues" (i.e., chastity, courtesy, discretion, humility, modesty, piety, submission, temperance) have been taught to young girls—must be delayed for another time. At the same time, the possibilities for inquiry to be found in the references of cited works are exciting; the education of girls and women—particularly as it has differed from the education of boys and men—is an area too little studied and perhaps even less understood. Since the study of education has for its research base work in nearly every discipline, the scope of the work to be done is broad, and its potential is nearly unlimited.

While there are a number of people who gave their time, effort, and enthusiasm to this project, I would especially like to thank Helena Miller and Michael Rockwood, without whose commitment to library research in the service of these ideas this volume would be greatly impoverished.

PART I

FOUNDATIONS FOR A STUDY OF
THE HISTORY OF WOMEN'S EDUCATION

PART I

FOUNDATIONS FOR A STUDY OF
THE HISTORY OF WOMEN'S EDUCATION

*Education is the means by which society prepares,
within the child, the essential conditions of its very
existence.*

—*Emile Durkheim*

Introduction

In 1969, Gerda Lerner observed that the relatively new field of
women's history needed a broader conceptual framework than that
provided by contemporary feminist historians of the subject. Rightly
concerned with discovering and rediscovering the lost story of
women's lives, they had defined women's history almost entirely in
terms of women's struggles against oppression (012). At the same
time, she suggested that the scope of studies in women's history be
somewhat more focused; the category "woman," she wrote, "is too vast
and diffuse to serve as a valid point of departure" (013, p. 10). In a
later essay (014, p. 158), she concludes that not only is the category
of "woman" too broad, but that no single conceptual framework is
sufficient to describe, analyze, and understand women's experience.
In the end, she thought, the study of women's history must eventuate
in a "reevaluation of the assumptions and methodology of traditional
history and traditional thought" (016, p. 180).

The study of the history of the education of women is just such
a focus within the more general category of women's history.
Scholars who have studied women's education have found that it is a
complex affair, one not easily categorized, and one which (like other
aspects of women's history) does not quite fit into more traditional
historical periods (010). Yet, the study of women's education is an
important aspect of history, because a society's attitudes, policies, and
practices related to the rearing of the next generation and the
continued intellectual and social development of its adult members
reflect some of that society's most fundamental values. An
understanding of those values helps us both to appreciate the past
and critique it in terms of the future. In addition, the nature of
education provided for any particular group within a society reveals a
good deal about the status and position of that group and in large

3

measure defines the social boundaries beyond which members of the group cannot easily move.

Until quite recently, the study of the education of girls and women has not been a high-priority topic among scholars of any discipline. In the past twenty years, however, a number of historians have focused on the ways in which education has served to influence women's lives and has been, in turn, influenced by women in their roles as wives, mothers, workers, civic activists, students and teachers. While a great deal of that story has yet to be told, there is enough to begin the synthesis that is necessary to provide frameworks for further work.

Scholarship on women's education falls generally into four categories. As might be expected, a major share of it has produced a record of inequities in the education of males and females, of ways in which girls and women have been denied access to the kind of education available to men. Emphasis in this work tends to be placed on formal instruction and/or schooling, and has provided us with an important rationale for studying women's education. It has also outlined the major beliefs and attitudes prevalent among males which served to prevent educational equity for females.

From this work we learn that—from the early Greeks to the day before yesterday—three major beliefs have intertwined to keep women from whatever was considered the "best" education of the time. These can be stated briefly as 1) the belief that women's intellect is inferior to men's; 2) the belief that women are fundamentally evil and that an educated woman is a danger to both individuals and society; and 3) the belief that, in any case, woman's role is such that she does not need formal education beyond the most rudimentary literacy. At least two assumptions underlie much of this kind of research, and make it at least somewhat problematic. One is that the term *education* is taken to mean formal schooling, and the other is that if females did not have access to the same education as males, they remained "uneducated."

A second type of historical inquiry has focused on rediscovering instances in which females *were* educated, either with males or separately. This work is of two kinds. First, it has provided us with material on "learned women," those few "special" women who through some combination of circumstances managed to acquire an education equivalent to the educated men of their time. Second, emphasis is placed on informal instruction that girls received in the home and shop, instruction aimed at preparing girls for expected roles as wives, mothers, mistresses of households, merchants, craftspeople, and so forth. In the first case, the work corresponds roughly with the "famous women" research in other historical areas, with the exception

that many of these women were only "famous" in their own time and
have since been lost to us. This work makes a major contribution,
because it rediscovers women who can serve as models of outstanding
achievement and provides a relatively clear understanding of the
ways in which new groups of people have gained access to educational
resources. It is necessary to remind ourselves, however, that
assumptions about the meaning of education in these cases differ
little from traditional ones, and thus do not teach us very much about
education in its broader sense as it affected and was affected by the
vast majority of women.

In the second case, research on women's "informal" education
provides us with the beginnings of a broader definition of education, a
definition necessary to understanding the actual complexity of the
educational enterprise. This kind of study regards the role played by
the family and other social institutions in educating females as a
primary rather than a secondary feature of women's educational
experience and opens the way for new kinds of educational research
more generally. It should be remembered that for most of history, no
one was formally educated to any great extent. Thus, the
examination of educational activities for women which occurred in
informal forms and in settings other than schools can illuminate
educational opportunities available to both males and females,
education which for the most part is ignored by educational
historians.

A third kind of historical research thus looks more explicitly at
the education of females in a broader context, suggesting that if
female education is to be truly understood, it must be studied in
terms of what Lawrence Cremin has called "educational
configurations" (006). Building on the work of Bernard Bailyn (001),
Cremin offers us a conceptual framework for redefining education to
include not only education as it occurs outside of formal schooling, but
also the ways in which individuals act to educate themselves, and the
ways in which institutions of education relate to one another in a
particular time and place. Thus, he defines education as "the
deliberate, systematic, and sustained effort to transmit, evoke, or
acquire knowledge, attitudes, values, skills, or sensibilities, as well as
any outcomes of that effort" (006, p. 27). In defining education this
way, Cremin moves from a distinction between formal education
(schooling) and informal education (everything else) and focuses on
education that is deliberate and organized no matter where it occurs.
Such a shift provides a framework that is especially useful in
studying the history of the education of women, since it legitimizes
education that occurs outside of schools, both in other institutional
settings and in individual and communitarian efforts in self

education. Moreover, because it casts a broad eye on the educational enterprise, this definition of education is more likely to take social context into account, and to emphasize differences in the education of girls and women according to social class and to the somewhat different consequences that historical events such as the spread of humanism, the Reformation, and the American Revolution have had on women's lives.

A configurational approach to the study of women's education also provides at least a partial solution to some of the problems that have been identified by critics of existing work. Cohen (005), for example, notes that historians of women's education often adopt very traditional views of education which focus on the development of the intellect, on education in the classics, and on schooling. Such emphasis excludes not only education for the roles women have traditionally played, but also—and perhaps more importantly—excludes how girls learned "to protect themselves, to deal with superiors, inferiors, and men in general, [and] to elicit help to get things done" (005, p. 154). Cohen also suggests that work on women's educational history should illuminate the differential outcomes of similar education for males and females in societies in which different roles for men and women are proscribed. Thus, for example, even when both sexes were taught Latin in the Middle Ages, it did not have the same meaning for males and females: "Whatever Latin offered men, it did not simply promise greater power or even unchallenged prestige to women" (005, p. 154).

Other critics point to a tendency among historians of women's education to neglect or ignore the profound impact of all-female educational activities and institutions. Palmieri (016), for example, cites American women's colleges as major sources of solidarity among some women in the late 19th and early 20th centuries (016, p. 540). She also criticizes a tendency to overemphasize certain cultural ideas as factors in women's education, particularly the notion that the "cult of domesticity" in 19th-century America precluded or distorted education for leadership. Such an over-emphasis, she notes, has caused some historians to conclude that women's colleges after the first generation "declined" in impact (016, p. 539). It may also prevent investigation into the educational role of women's participation in social reform movements, as well as into similarities and differences between women's colleges and men's colleges in common eras (016, p. 540).

In general, stress on higher education in the literature on women's educational history has been criticized in terms of its propensity to ignore the rich diversity of educational experiences among women of different classes and among women of color, as well as its neglect of elementary and secondary schooling, and the role of the family and of religion in providing academic and other kinds of instruction for women. A further criticism of the general literature on women's education has to do with problems of source material on plans for the education of women. Jardine, for example, argues that many of these sources are either too optimistic or too pessimistic in terms of their conclusions about women's educational experiences:

> On the one hand we are likely to find generous and confident extension of opportunities for education (secular and religious) and for partnership (outside and inside the home) from those who take it for granted that the women they address themselves to will observe due moderation in their pursuit of these goals.... But on the other hand, those who already felt the oppressive presence of a "new order," "the world turned upside down,"—the moralist and social satirist—are almost inevitably going to seize on unfamiliar opportunities for women as yet another example of the misguided attitudes of the times (008, p. 39).

The point, of course, is that it is always necessary to remember that the education of women was and is not a single, monolithic experience but is shaped by time, place, status, opportunity, and individual and collective endeavor.

Finally, a fourth set of work on women's educational history—fairly new and as yet small—assumes that the study of women's education can provide models which will benefit education more generally. This work goes beyond the simple *inclusion* of women's education in educational history and asks how the study of women's educational experience can give us direction not only for transforming our historical ideas but also for recreating educational practice in the present and future (017).

While this book is primarily about the education of women in the United States, the roots of that education lie deep in the history of Western Civilization. Thus, the considerable work on the education of women in western Europe, from Greece to about the 18th century, provides a foundation for our current interests. As Robert Frost noted, we are a nation of immigrants, and our ideas about education came with us from other lands. To be sure, the American experience has shaped and reshaped these ideas; but it is always well to know something about the original sources of our current knowledge and attitudes. Taken together, the literature on the education of women in Europe offers the reader some general themes

in women's education, themes which are remarkable in their
persistence even to the present day. These do not by any means
provide an all-inclusive picture of women's education, but they do
suggest questions which as yet have not often been asked and which
certainly have not been definitively answered.

BIBLIOGRAPHY

001.   Bailyn, Bernard. *Education in the Forming of American
        Society: Needs and Opportunities for Study.* Chapel Hill:
        University of North Carolina Press, 1960.

002.   Beard, Mary R. *Women as a Force in History.* New York:
        Collier Books, 1962.

003.   Boulding, Elise. *The Underside of History: A View of Women
        Through Time.* Boulder, CO: Westview Press, 1976.

004.   Clifford, Geraldine Joncich. "History as Experience: The Uses
        of Personal-History Documents in the History of
        Education." *History of Education 7* (1978): 183-196.

005.   Cohen, Elizabeth S. "On Doing the History of Women's
        Education." Review of *Better than Rubies: A History of
        Women's Education,* by Phyllis Stock. *History of
        Education Quarterly 19* (1979): 151-155.

006.   Cremin, Lawrence A. *Public Education and the Education of
        the Public.* New York: Basic Books, 1976.

007.   Graham, Patricia Albjerg. "So Much to Do: Guides for
        Historical Research on Women in Higher Education."
        Teachers College Record 76 (1975): 421-429.

008.   Jardine, Lisa. "The Double Bind of Renaissance Education
        and Reformed Religion." In *Still Harping on Daughters:
        Women and Drama in the Age of Shakespeare,* pp. 37-67.
        Totowa, NJ: Barnes and Noble, 1983.

009.   Kelly-Gadol, Joan. "The Social Relations of the Sexes:
        Methodological Implications of Women's History." *Signs:
        Journal of Women in Culture and Society 1* (1976):
        809-823.

010.   Kelly, Joan. *Women, History and Theory*. Chicago: University of Chicago Press, 1984.

011.   Lagemann, Ellen Condliffe. "Women's History." In John H. Best, ed., *Historical Inquiry in Education*, pp. 251-264. Washington, DC: AERA, 1983.

012.   Lerner, Gerda. "New Approaches to the Study of Women in American History." In *The Majority Finds Its Past*, pp. 3-14. New York: Oxford University Press, 1979.

013.   ———. "Placing Women in History: Definitions and Challenges." In *The Majority Finds Its Past*, pp. 145-159. New York: Oxford University Press, 1979.

014.   ———. "The Challenge of Women's History." In *The Majority Finds Its Past*, pp. 168-180. New York: Oxford University Press, 1979.

015.   ———. "Black Women in the U.S.: A Problem in Historiography and Interpretation." In *The Majority Finds Its Past*, pp. 63-82. New York: Oxford University Press, 1979.

016.   Palmieri, Patricia A. "Paths and Pitfalls: Illuminating Woman's Educational History." *Harvard Educational Review 49* (1979): 447-541.

017.   Rury, John. "Education in the New Women's History." *Educational Studies 17* (1986): 1-15.

018.   Scott, Joan W. "Is Gender a Useful Category of Historical Analysis?" *American Historical Review 91* (1986): 1053-1075.

CHAPTER 1

European Themes in the Education of Women

There is a good principle which created order, light, and man, and an evil principle which created chaos, darkness, and woman.
—Pythagoras

From the time of the early Greeks, women's educational experiences in Europe show a remarkable similarity across time and culture. While individual experiences vary greatly—there is, for example, a fundamental difference between the education of the medieval abbess and the peasant girl, or between the Renaissance lady and the 15th-century shop girl—the educational lives of women share major themes which were carried across the sea to the new world and are evident still in the United States. In the following chapters, these themes will be articulated in greater detail; for now, they are presented in outline as major threads in the historical tapestry of women's educational experience.

Prevailing Attitudes Toward Educating Women

Although the continuing expansion of women's education is clear, it is also the case that *male attitudes toward the schooling of women have historically been negative.* Two relatively short but succinct articles by Clabaugh (020) and Smith (031) indicate the main rationales which underlie much of the misogyny regarding women's education. First, it has generally been felt that women were intellectually inferior to men. This belief might be stated in categorical terms, as Socrates does when he says, "All of the pursuits of men are the pursuits of women also, but in all of them a woman is inferior to a man" (020, p. 130). Or, as Aristotle put it: "The male is by nature superior and the female inferior, the male ruler and the female subject" (031, p. 5). On the other hand, it might be presented as a kind of puzzled observation of a natural phenomenon. Erasmus, for example, writes: "I do not know the reason, but just as a saddle is not suitable for an ox, so learning is unsuitable for women" (020, p. 128).

Second, if the presence of erudite and competent women in every era seemed to make the first argument less than rock-solid, it was presumed that since women's place was very definitely in the home, intellectual learning was not necessary. Indeed, such an education might very well make women dissatisfied with their lives, impatient with men, and quite possibly even unable to conceive. Kant, for example, notes that "Even if a woman excels in arduous learning and painstaking thinking, they will exterminate the merits of her sex" (020, p. 133). And, even in the 20th century, the President of Stanford University felt constrained to write that "There is not the slightest evidence that highly educated women are necessarily rendered sterile or celibate by their education" (656, Solomon, p. 59).

A variation of the second argument plays down the role of women as homemakers, focusing instead on their role as pleasant companions and/or inspirations to men. Goethe, for example, claims that "We love things other than the intellect in a young woman. We love what is beautiful, confiding, teaching, youthful in her; her character, her faults, her whims, and God knows what other undefinable things, but we do not love her intellect" (020, p. 134).

And finally, if none of the above arguments were sufficient to prevent the formal education of women, the belief that women were inherently evil was used to justify the absence of education on the grounds that such learning would only enhance their destructive power (020, 031).

Although such arguments have lost some of their power over the centuries, Smith (031) asserts that they are alive and well and among us still. Currently dressed in the garb of scientific empiricism, they appear in studies that show deficits among girls in quantitative and spatial tasks which are attributed to "natural" differences. Many still believe that girls are more intuitive and boys more logical by nature rather than by socialization and training.

Nevertheless, *there have always been men who advocated academic or classical instruction for girls.* Despite a pervasive set of attitudes that would deny academic instruction for girls and women, there have always been men for whom the evidence of their eyes and ears was a powerful incentive to provide for and assist in the education of their daughters and—occasionally—their sisters and wives. Clearly, for some, women did not constitute a lesser species when it came to the enhancement of their intellectual capacities. One of the earliest of these was, of course, Plato, who, in his plan for the education of the female Guardians, set forth the notion that sex was a difference that made no difference in education.

Somewhat unusual among his Roman peers, the Stoic philosopher Seneca thought that women were capable of wisdom and learning (047). Although his writing reveals a traditional view of women's place as in the home, he also opposed a double standard of behavior for men and women, sought to treat them intellectually as he treated men, and was "willing to grant them equal opportunity at the banquet table, equal place at the feast of human endeavor" (047, p. 157).

A number of men over the centuries have proposed detailed plans for the education of women, including St. Jerome's instructions for teaching reading and writing to the child Paula, Abelard's rule for the education of the nuns at the Paraclete, and Pierre DuBois' plan for the education of boys and girls to prepare them for missionary duty in the Middle East during the Crusades (057). Considerable attention was given to the education of women during the Renaissance and among the Humanists of the 15th and 16th centuries, and many established schools and/or themselves taught young girls.

No matter how well they succeeded in acquiring formal education, *women have generally been excluded from whatever education was perceived to be of the most value at any particular time and place.* Education for women has historically been used to separate the spheres in which the sexes operated. One way in which this has been expressed is through the practice of providing women certain kinds of education but denying them the particular kind of education that has been thought to be the special province of men and thus automatically of higher status or value. Another way has been to include women in "male" educational activities but for very different reasons.

Much has been made, for example, of the Spartan practice of including women in the physical education that was so much a part of Greek instruction. The purpose of physical education for women in Sparta, however, was to ensure a healthy pool of child-bearers to provide the next generation of warriors (037).

Similarly, while both males and females have frequently been taught to read, instruction in writing was often offered only to males. One of the results of this practice has been that women are prepared to read tracts instructing them on their "proper" role but not prepared to write tracts of their own.

Historical examples abound in which women have been excluded from the sort of education thought suitable for men: philosophy in Greece, government in Rome, medicine in the later Middle Ages, and science and mathematics from the Enlightenment to the present day. When women did acquire such knowledge, they were frequently ridiculed as "unwomanly" (or burned as witches) or their work was attributed to fathers, brothers, or husbands (019).

At certain times, the nature of education thought appropriate for men changed so that it became appropriate for women but not for men. Thus, for example, in the Middle Ages when a great deal of political consolidation was achieved through warfare, liberal education in philosophy and the arts came to be thought of as effeminate for men when compared to military education. "Real" men didn't read, they fought.

No matter what forms it took in different periods of history, this differential education for women created and recreated a separation between the sexes based on social roles and eventuated in a status hierarchy which placed and maintained women in a subordinate position.

One result of this exclusion is that *many of the major historical events which are often cited as improving the cultural and educational prospects for all people have, in fact, had correspondingly limiting consequences for women.* Western educational history is ordinarily thought of as, in some sense, the story of progress characterized by increasing education and enlightenment. Landmarks on that amazing march are often given: the rise of the university, the emergence of guilds, the shift to humanism, the invention of the printing press, and the development of science as the way of knowing *par excellence.* When one is studying the education of women, however, a somewhat different picture emerges. Women's education, for example, has been cyclical, rather than progressing in anything close to a straight line. Periods in which formal education was available that would enable women to participate in public life have come and gone with a regularity that might give contemporary women pause to consider their own fate.

In part, women's educational experience has been closely related to their experience in other aspects of life. When general consensus allowed women relative freedom to participate in life outside the home, so education in terms of formal instruction in a curriculum shared by boys and men was also allowed. Unfortunately, in many of the periods often associated with the "liberation" of humanity, women became increasingly restricted. Thus, for example, Kelly has noted that the Renaissance—notable for a flowering of the human spirit that depended a great deal on the availability of a liberal education—was a time in which women's lives were increasingly restricted (081).

So it is that the rise of the university spelled the death-knell for available education for many girls in the convent schools (as well as providing the beginning of the end of women's role as healers). The emergence of guilds eventually resulted in restrictions on women's employment and the education provided within the guild. And the emergence of humanism, while it did foster increased attention to the education of women among major humanist thinkers, also put women in a kind of double bind. Jardine notes that while women were encouraged to acquire learning, they were vilified if that learning were used in any but the most traditional roles (008).

Similarly, Fraser (097) notes that the 17th century, which could have framed women's education in the aftermath of major contributions by humanist thinkers, witnessed instead a sharp decline in the availability of advanced education. Thus, a survey of the history of women's education in Europe engenders both excitement and a sense of frustration: excitement because we learn that there have been periods in which women could and did claim amazing educational achievements; but frustration when one realizes how easily such education could be used to "keep women in their place" or the extent to which it could disappear altogether.

Women's Access to Formal Education

When talking about women's access to formal education, it is important to remember that *social class has determined to a large degree both the access of girls and women to education and the kind of education they received.* Although elementary literacy and an introduction to arithmetic and music were probably more available than we might suppose, in fact, we are not sure how many girls in any era were able to take advantage of them. We do know that from early Greece to the present day, upper-class girls and young women have had opportunities for schooling unknown to the working class and the poor. Furthermore, until quite recently even among the elite, girls' education frequently depended on the inclination of fathers to educate their daughters, on the presence of brothers for whom tutors were engaged and books and materials provided, or on the accidental fact that they were only children or born into families with no sons (057).

The absence of schooling, or even the absence of literacy, however, does not mean that girls received no education at all. All education, as Stock (032) correctly describes it,

> has a social rather than individual function. The aim of
> the educator is to produce an adult who will play a
> certain desired role in society. . . . [Moreover], the
> education of the two sexes [often] reflects actual social

and power relationships between men and women in the
society (pp. 12-13).

From the point of view of those (nearly always men) who have
had the power to make decisions regarding women's education (and
not infrequently, from the perspective of women themselves who
obediently internalize social values), the "desired role in society" for
women has almost invariably been that of wife, mother, and manager
of the household. It is therefore not surprising that the education of
girls and women has been primarily devoted toward that end. Even
when upper-class girls received advanced intellectual education, the
purpose was primarily to help them become better companions to
husbands in leadership roles. In general, the lower the class to which
a girl belongs, the more narrowly vocational her education has been.
Nevertheless, *formal education, including but not limited to
schooling, in elementary reading, writing, arithmetic, and music has
been available to at least some girls since the fourth century B.C.*
Despite a disinclination to educate girls and women, at least some
girls of nearly every class have received formal instruction in
elementary subjects for over 2,000 years. Pomeroy (049) notes that
terracotta figurines from a wide range of locations in Greece show
girls reading and writing and some even suggest girls carrying their
writing tablets to school. There is considerable debate among
classical scholars on the position of women in ancient Greece; most
assert that in part because the common marriage age for girls was 14
or 15, respectable women received only sufficient education to engage
in domestic tasks and that such education was given not only by
mothers, but also by husbands (042). Other interpretations of existing
evidence, however, suggest that from the end of the fourth century,
B.C., some women had access to and took advantage of at least an
elementary education and sometimes more advanced learning. It is
known, for example, that the Pythagorean schools admitted girls
(039), and girls in Sparta received a publicly sponsored education and
enjoyed a degree of freedom of expression higher than their Athenian
sisters (037).
Elementary schooling for some girls has been a fact of life in
all the centuries since, although the form of that schooling has varied
considerably. One of the few scholars to take a broad view of
education in terms of its many aspects and settings, Kersey notes that
at various periods, deliberate instruction was offered in schools by
professional teachers, at home by mothers, tutors and governesses, in
monasteries and convents, in castles and at court, in shops and
workshops in the form of apprenticeships, and even in hospitals and
alms-houses (061). Except in the case of some convents during the

early and later Middle Ages, elementary education was designed for children of both sexes, and when girls and boys have been schooled together, the curriculum has most often been the same. German Protestant reformers in the 16th century developed folk schools in order to provide a basic education to both boys and girls, elevating that goal to legal status in many cases (098).

Three points should be made about elementary education during most of Western history. First, the vast majority of all children received only a rudimentary formal education. Many did not attend any school at all, but were taught what they needed to know by parents and apprentice masters. Second, as Monter (100) points out, literacy does not precisely equal education. Nor does literacy necessarily mean reading *and* writing, but may have meant reading only, especially for girls. Third, because scholars of women's history have so often defined "education" as higher or advanced learning, we still have much to learn about the nature and consequences of elementary education. We do not know, for example, the degree of intellectual content involved in socialization processes outside the school (068). Moreover, when the majority of people received no formal education at all, an elementary education was perhaps of more significance than it implies today.

Still, over the centuries, *there have always been exceptions to the rule—"learned women" who defied convention.* In part because there have been men interested in the academic or classical instruction of women, in all ages there have been certain women whose education in advanced studies was as good as or better than their male contemporaries. Almost always among the elite of their respective societies, these "learned women" were often admired and wielded considerable power. The exact number of such women is difficult to determine either because records are sparse or because germane materials have not yet been examined. Indirect evidence sometimes, however, indicates that there were more highly schooled women in a given society than we may imagine. Gomme (042), for example, suggests that the frequency and degree of verbal abuse used by the Greek playwrights in describing the learned woman may be possible evidence that there were sufficient numbers of them to cause distress among the misogynists.

In the Middle Ages, a number of women—usually through the Church—acquired classical educations that rivaled and surpassed their male contemporaries. The list of famous and powerful abbesses who served as educational, political, literary, and social leaders of their times in England, Germany, and France is a long one. While many of these women remain unfamiliar to most of us (usually because their names and achievements have not yet penetrated the history books we normally study), the stories of the German nun and playwright Roswitha, the English queen Eleanor of Aquitaine, the French poet Marie de France, the English mystic Hildegard of Bingen, and the French intellectual Héloise are beginning to be told until their lives are woven into contemporary thought.

If the Middle Ages produced a number of "learned women," the rise of humanism opened more doors to education for increasing numbers of upper- and middle-class girls. Indeed, their numbers increased sufficiently that they became identifiable as a class or group, leading as always to debates about the "usefulness" and propriety of educating them at all. Humanists in the 15th and 16th centuries had less trouble with the notion that women had the intellectual capacity for higher learning. Indeed, many thought that women should be able to read the "great works" in the original, and thus they promoted the notion that women should learn Latin and Greek. They did so, however, in the belief that such an education would produce "better" women who could more easily satisfy the requirements of marriage to successful and well-educated husbands. Thus, while the men who advocated higher learning for women did increase access to formal education for women, they also took the control of women's education away from mothers and women's communities, and became the arbiters of what an educated woman should be. Furthermore, the education designed for women was aimed in traditional directions; only the level of instruction and content was expanded.

Many women who acquired advanced education did so at some cost, and *the price paid by these "learned women" has been high in exclusion from both the society of men and the society of women.* In general terms, despite periods in which classical instruction has been advocated for women, the position of the "learned woman" in society at any given time has been an uncomfortable one. Frequently, then as now, part of the discomfort came from having to choose between the pursuit of higher learning or the pursuit of marriage. King (084), for example, notes that at adulthood women were faced with "a choice between two futures: marriage and full participation in social life on the one hand; or abstention from marriage and withdrawal from the world. . . . To marry implied the abandonment of beloved studies" (084, pp. 68-69).

Most women who had studied a classical curriculum as young girls abandoned such study in favor of marriage and its inevitable consequence, motherhood. Those that did not make this choice suffered exclusion from both the world of women and the world of men. Their sexual identity was often questioned by both sexes as being "beyond nature" (084, p. 78). Many men, somehow threatened by the prospect of a woman competitor in the realm of learned studies, berated them as "warrior women . . . Amazons of intellect" (084, p. 79). King writes movingly about this phenomenon:

> [Men's attitude toward] the learned woman, whose learning destroyed the integrity of her sexual identity [created for them] a fitting image: that of the armed maiden, a fusion of the icons of Thena, the chaste goddess of wisdom, and of the Amazons, fierce warriors ruthless to men. . . . And behind these visions of female warriors lay the vision of Athena, martially armed, unnaturally born, coldly virginal, and though female, defined not by sex but by intellect. The chill refinement of the symbol of wisdom coalesced with the ferocity of the Amazons" (084, pp. 79-80).

The equation of the highly educated woman with a fierce and cold nature (and often, an ugly visage) continues to work its damage on women in the 20th century. Perhaps the best example is the case of Rosalind Franklin, a co-discoverer with James Watson and Francis Crick of the structure of DNA. Working in England, Franklin was an expert on crystallography, and had been working in the lab to which Watson came prior to his arrival. In his story of the discovery of the double helix, however, Watson does not give Franklin the slightest credit; rather, he reports that she was "nervous," and "tense" and wonders, as he listens to her lectures, "how she would look if she took off her glasses and did something novel with her hair."[1]

The degree to which the "learned woman" has been ridiculed and denied her sexual identity may be discerned, in part, from the somewhat extreme cases of women who—seeking to acquire advanced learning, especially in the professions, in the face of discrimination and defamation—disguised themselves as men in order to obtain university educations (071). In general, however, the "learned woman" has had to go against the grain of cultural norms in order to pursue a love of learning, and the price has been both loneliness and vilification.

---

[1]James D. Watson. *The Double Helix*. New York: New American Library, 1968.

Religion and Education for the Role of Wife and Mother

Regardless of the nature of the knowledge imparted to girls, the teachers who taught them, or the settings in which they learned, *both formal and informal education for women has been most often valued in the degree to which it has provided the necessary background for their lives in the home.* Central to this kind of education, and of obvious importance in maintaining the separation of public and private worlds, has been socialization to such "feminine virtues" as humility, sweetness, simplicity, peaceableness, kindness, piety, temperance, obedience, patience, charitableness, chastity, modesty, constancy, and conformity (083). In addition, the development of skills in spinning, needlework, weaving, food production, cookery, housekeeping, sewing, child-rearing, and the raising of medicinal herbs and practice of family medicine has traditionally been part of the deliberate instruction of girls. To the extent that the ability to read, write, and cipher has been thought necessary to these "womanly" tasks, it has been either condoned or encouraged.

Frequently, major events such as wars created the conditions under which certain knowledge and skills usually associated with men became necessary for women. Christine de Pizan, for example, suggested that women should know how to keep financial records and be familiar with legal affairs, as well as be knowledgeable about military defenses, since during the Hundred Years' War women were often left in charge of the home, estate, or castle (073).

The importance of organized religion in the education of women can hardly be underestimated. *Religious institutions and the belief that women were more suited to the spread of religious knowledge played a significant part in education for girls and women throughout most of history.* Deliberate education was an institutionalized practice in early Greece (044) among women's religious cults devoted to "women's" poetry, and to "the sensual education and affirmation of upper-class young women" (p. 458). In the Middle Ages, the church was the primary institution of education for children and young people of both sexes and of particular importance for the education of girls and young women. The great convent schools provided systematic instruction in literacy as well as in religion and some of the fine arts to girls of the noble classes and were almost the only source of education for girls of the lower classes (032, p. 69). Indeed, from the 8th to the 12th centuries, religious schools produced nearly all the powerful women who were an integral part of the social, political, and intellectual life of the period in Europe, for they offered the opportunity not only to learn but also to teach. Nuns were usually daughters of the upper classes who often became not only the teachers of the children in the schools, but also taught one another. It is clear that some of these women achieved scholastic excellence as well as positions of power within the church as abbesses and administrators of major monastic orders. With the rise of the university in the 12th century, however, the importance of the convent school declined, and with that decline the availability of formal education for girls was nearly lost.

During the Reformation, particularly in Germany, the church once again became a proponent of the education of girls. This time, however, it was the Protestant church, which encouraged the education of "future mothers" so that they could promulgate the new religion to their children (098). Thus, throughout history, the church has not only provided educational activities and an avenue of scholarship to women, it has also in large measure defined the purpose of that education in terms of women's traditional roles.

Apart from religious instruction, it is the case that *for most of history, mothers have been considered important teachers.* One of the consequences of the emergence of the school as the central agency of education and the professionalization of teaching that has been a characteristic of the 20th century is a diminution of the perception that mothers have valuable knowledge to offer their children. If anything, 20th century beliefs have centered on expectations that the mother would prepare her children to behave well in school, but avoid trying to "teach" them anything that they might better learn in the classroom. For most of history, this has not been the case. Indeed, the role of the mother in the education of her children has been one of the most important rationales for educating women at all.

It is reasonable, of course, to assume that when very few children went to school, when, in fact, schools were relatively unnecessary to the pursuit of earning a living, most education would be offered at home. Much of this kind of education was in the form of apprenticeship; for boys in a trade, and for girls in the homemaking arts. However, the role of the mother in primary literacy and in building interests and habits of thought and behavior that would serve sons well as leaders has always been an important one. While this was not quite as true in early Greece, it seems to have been very definitely the case in Rome, where the family was the basic unit of the political structure and where women had charge of their sons at least until they were seven.

An example of such a mother is Cornelia, whose sons Tiberius and Gaius Grachus became major figures in 2nd century Rome, and who "was admired for her virtue, fidelity and, not least, her intelligence" (036, p. 131), which she put to good use in supervising the education of her twelve children. Slaves in the homes of wealthy Romans also were given decent educations so that they could assist in supervising the education of the children of the house.

Examples of the importance of mothers as teachers abound in the literature on education, not only with respect to their roles in direct teaching but also in the ways in which they provided books for their children's tutelage. Bell (055) has written a particularly interesting study of women as book owners during the Middle Ages, showing that it was primarily women who bought and kept libraries of books, some of which were destined for the edification of children. In fact, what Bell calls the "special relationship" of women to books was, in part, because of their role as educators of their children.

Even 16th century humanism, which advocated a higher classical education for many women, did so in terms of its ability to enhance women's roles as mothers and moral agents in the family. Humanist thought in the 15th and 16th centuries was concerned, among other things, with virtue and that concern was a key to interest in educating women (078). Not interested in altering women's place in society, the humanists nevertheless believed that a woman educated in the "best of Western thought" would be a *better* wife and mother.

Women's Efforts to Educate Themselves

The story of women's education is not only the story of what women were *allowed* to learn, or even what they *did* learn as a part of growing up. It is also the story of women's efforts to support one another in intellectual pursuits. Thus, *there have always been communities of women dedicated to knowledge, learning, and teaching.* Not all who acquired advanced learning, however, had to do so in isolation or by exercising a singular determination. In each of the major historical periods with which we are familiar, there existed communities of women whose major purpose was to encourage the development of education for their sisters. Some of these communities are the subject of considerable debate, often revolving around their function in the society. It is known that both Sappho and Aspasia in ancient Greece founded schools for girls in which communities of women aided in the instructional process and provided support for girls and young women (039). Both of these women, however, have often been vilified by historians—Sappho as a lesbian and Aspasia as an interfering scold in the political life of Periclean Athens. Similarly, the community of early Greek women known as the Hetairai has been variously described as composed of "the only educated women in Athens" (038) and as a coterie of women of low reputation (048). Education obtained by women in convents and abbeys during the early years of the Middle Ages has already been mentioned and serves as another example of women's communities that helped to keep educational activities alive for girls and women. Somewhat later in the Middle Ages, the beguines of the late 12th and 13th centuries stand out as yet another community of women devoted to serving the poor, aiding the homeless and teaching. The beguines lived in semi-monastic communities, leading religious but not secluded lives. They did not take the vows of nuns but maintained ties of service to the urban communities in which they lived. Often unmarried women and widows from the middle- and upper-middle classes, many of the beguines had the advantages of early education in their homes but could find neither the employment afforded to working-class girls and peasants nor space in a convent. Thus, they banded together in loosely-knit communities, forming a network of service throughout France, Germany, and the Low Countries. Distrusted in some circles (often the Church itself) as women independent of much visible supervision by religious or secular authorities, the beguines were persecuted in some areas for heresy, laziness, or illegal begging. Nevertheless, they continued their work for more than a century, and were memorialized in 1328 as "so circumspect in their manners and so learned in household matters, that great and honorable people send their daughters to them to be brought up, hoping that to whatever state of life they are afterwards called, they will be better prepared than others" (062, p. 119).

Two 18th-century examples of communities of women that served to encourage and support the pursuit of learning and public involvement are the French and English salon movements. These institutions are nearly unique in the history of women's education—as, indeed, they are in intellectual history. Serving as an "informal university" (101, p. 185) for women, the salons were, in a sense, intellectual "parties," invitational gatherings in private homes where women "could exchange ideas, avail themselves of some of the best minds of their time, receive and give criticism, read their own works and hear the works of others, and, in general, pursue in their own way some form of higher education" (101, p. 185).

At a time when women were still considered intellectually inferior to men, the salon was an ingenious construction that allowed at least some women the opportunity to learn and to participate in the public debates of the day while still "playing" the acceptable role of hostess. The French salon, moreover, served as a kind of apprenticeship training for younger women, who assisted the established salonière in planning and carrying out the preparations and activities of the salon. By the middle of the 18th century, the

French salon was an established institution, "*the* major channel of communication among intelligent people of means with enough leisure to enjoy its benefits. It served as newspaper, journal, literary society, and university" (101, p. 186).

Coming into existence somewhat later than the French salons, the English salon movement was created on a somewhat different pattern. Called "Bluestockings," members of the upper-middle class English movement formed a network of friendships which came to exclude men; indeed, they often criticized their French sisters as being too intent on "pleasure" and not serious enough about study. Perhaps because they specifically did not masquerade behind a facade of "hostessing," the Blues were frequently ridiculed as vain, pretentious, and unfeminine. Nevertheless, both the French and English salons provided an opportunity for women to support one another while engaging in the kind of intellectual activities often denied them elsewhere.

Finally, *the education of women, particularly higher learning, has been an effective stimulus to women's rebellion against misogyny that has fueled demands for still further education for women.* Some "communities" of women did not exist in a common geographical space, but have been considered communities nevertheless by historians of women's education and work. One of these, referred to as the *querelle des femmes* by Kelly-Gadol (082) and Fox-Genovese (021), consists of women who, over a period of 400 years, created the arguments for women's education in a series of essays, tracts, and letters. Beginning with Christine de Pisan in the 14th century and ending with Mary Wollstonecraft in the 18th, these women could be called early feminists, although they thought of themselves only as defenders and proponents of women. United in their attacks on misogyny, these primarily European women (Anne Hutchinson in the 17th century American colonies was a kindred spirit) wrote polemical works in response to "specific, published attacks on them" (082, p. 66). In addition, they wrote in terms of gender rather than sex, understanding the social construction rather than the biological basis of attitudes toward women (083, p. 67).

The *querelle* is only one example of a group of women who, having obtained some education, used it to analyze women's place in the general society, to fight against the mistreatment of women, and to demand access to education and position in the public world. Not attacking men so much as the male bias in their respective cultures, women from Sappho to Steinem have observed that education is a fundamental key to opening the door to equality and equity for women. Nothing less than a full consideration of women's education in the context of current social conditions (whatever they may be in any given time or place) will serve to separate women from their traditional roles, redefine women's place, and reconceptualize a more humane society.

BIBLIOGRAPHY

General Works

019. Alic, Margaret. *Hypatia's Heritage: A History of Women In Science.* Boston: Beacon Press, 1986.

020. Clabaugh, Gary K. "A History of Male Attitudes Toward Educating Women." *Educational Horizons 64* (1986): 127-135.

021. Fox-Genovese, Elizabeth. "Culture and Consciousness in the Intellectual History of European Women." *Signs: Journal of Women in Culture and Society 12* (1987): 493-547.

022. Gardiner, Dorothy. *English Girlhood at School: A Study of Women's Education through Twelve Centuries.* London: Oxford University Press, 1929.

023. Hodgson, Gerald. *Studies in French Education from Rabelais to Rousseau.* Cambridge: University Press, 1908.

024. Hurd-Mead, Kate Campbell. *A History of Women in Medicine.* Haddam, CT: The Haddam Press, 1938.

025. Kamm, Josephine. *Hope Deferred: Girls' Education in English History.* London: Methune and Co., 1965.

026. Kersey, Shirley. *Classics in the Education of Girls and Women.* Metuchen, NJ: The Scarecrow Press, 1981.

027. Labalme, Patricia H., ed. *Beyond Their Sex: Learned Women of the European Past.* New York: New York University Press, 1980.

028. Lange, Helene. *Higher Education of Women in Europe.* Trans., L. R. Klemm. New York: 1890.

029.   Prince, Martha (Trans.) *History of the Education of Women in France.* Paris: Didier and Co., 1883.

030.   Schiebinger, Londa. "The History and Philosophy of Women in Science: A Review Essay." *Signs: Journal of Women in Culture and Society 12* (1987): 305-332.

031.   Smith, L. Glenn. "From Plato to Jung: Centuries of Educational Inequities." *Educational Horizons 60* (1981): 4-10.

032.   Stock, Phyllis. *Better Than Rubies: A History of Women's Education.* New York: Putnam, 1978.

033.   Yoshi, Kasuya. *A Complete Study of the Secondary Education of Girls in England, Germany and the United States.* New York: 1933.

034.   Zuelow, Margo J. "Highlights in the History of the Education of Women." Paper presented at the 4th Statewide Conference of the University of Alaska Community Colleges, Fairbanks, Alaska, May 15, 1983. ERIC: ED 237 417.

Greece and Rome

035.   Balsdon, J.P.V.D. *Roman Women: Their History and Habits.* London: Bodley Head, 1962.

036.   Best, E. E. "Cicero, Livy, and Educated Roman Women." *Classical Journal 65* (1970): 199-204.

037.   Cartledge, Paul. "Spartan Wives: Liberation or License?" *Classical Quarterly 75* (1981): 84-105.

038.   Donaldson, James. *Woman: Her Position and Influence in Ancient Greece and Rome, and Among the Early Christians.* London: Longmans, Green, and Co., 1907.

039.   Durant, Will. *The Life of Greece.* New York: Simon and Schuster, 1939.

040.   Finley, M. I. "The Silent Women of Rome." *Horizon 7* (1965): 57-64.

041.   Foley, Helene P., ed. *Reflections of Women in Antiquity*. New York: Gordon and Breach Science Publishers, 1981.

042.   Gomme, A. W. "The Position of Women in Athens in the Fifth and Fourth Centuries B.C." *Classical Philology 20* (1925): 1-25.

043.   Hadas, Moses. "Observations on Athenian Women." *Classical Weekly 39* (1936): 97-100.

044.   Hallett, Judith P. "Sappho and Her Social Context: Sense and Sensuality." *Signs: Journal of Women in Culture and Society 4* (1979): 447-464.

045.   Lefkowitz, Mary and Fant, M. B. *Women's Life in Greece and Rome*. Rev. ed. Baltimore: Johns Hopkins University Press, 1986.

046.   MacMullen, Ramsey. "Women in Public in the Roman Empire." *Historia 29* (1980): 209-218.

047.   Motto, A. L. "Seneca on Women's Liberation." *Classical World 65* (1972): 155-157.

048.   Pomeroy, Sarah. *Goddesses, Whores, Wives and Slaves: Women in Classical Antiquity*. New York: Schocken Books, 1976.

049.   ———. "Technai kai mousai: The Education of Women in the Fourth Century and in the Hellenistic Period." *American Journal of Ancient History 2* (1977): 51-68.

050.   Richter, Donald C. "The Position of Women in Classical Athens." *Classical Journal 67* (1971): 1-8.

051.   Seltman, Charles. "The Status of Women in Athens." *Greece and Rome, Series 2* (1955): 119-124.

052.   ———. *Women in Antiquity*. London: Thames and Hudson, 1956.

053.   Zinserling, Verena. *Women in Greece and Rome*. New York: Abner Schram, 1973.

The Middle Ages

054.   Abrams, Annie. "Women Traders in Medieval London."
       Economic Journal 26 (1916): 276-85.

055.   Bell, Susan Groag. "Medieval Women Book Owners: Arbiters
       of Lay Piety and Ambassadors of Culture." *Signs:
       Journal of Women in Culture and Society 7* (1982): 742-
       768.

056.   Erickson, Carolly. "The Vision of Women." In *The Medieval
       Vision*, Ch. 8. New York: Oxford University Press, 1976.

057.   Ferrante, Joan M. "The Education of Women in the Middle
       Ages in Theory, Fact, and Fantasy." In Patricia H.
       Labalme, ed., *Beyond Their Sex: Learned Women of the
       European Past*, pp. 9-42. New York: New York
       University Press, 1980.

058.   Harksen, Sibylle. *Women in the Middle Ages*. New York:
       Abner Schram, 1975.

059.   Heinrich, Sister Mary Pia. *The Cannonesses and Education in
       the Early Middle Ages*. Washington, DC: Catholic
       University of America, 1924.

060.   Kemp-Welch, Alice. *Of Six Mediaeval Women*. London:
       Macmillan and Co., 1913.

061.   Kersey, Shirley. "Medieval Education of Girls and Women."
       Educational Horizons 58 (1980): 188-192.

062.   Labarge, Margaret Wade. *A Small Sound of the Trumpet:
       Women in Medieval Life*. Boston: Beacon Press, 1986.

063.   Lehrman, Sara. "The Education of Women in the Middle
       Ages." In Douglas Radcliffe-Umstead, ed., *The Roles and
       Images of Women in the Middle Ages and Renaissance*,
       pp. 133-144. Pittsburgh: Center for Medieval and
       Renaissance Studies, 1975.

064.   Leibell, Helen Dominica. "Anglo-Saxon Education of Women:
       From Hilda to Hildegarde." (Ph.D. diss., Georgetown
       University), 1922.

065.   Lucas, Angela M. *Women in the Middle Ages: Religion, Marriage, and Letters.* New York: St. Martin's Press, 1983.

066.   Orme, Nicholas. *English Schools in the Middle Ages.* London: 1973.

067.   Posten, M. M., ed. *Medieval Women.* Cambridge: Cambridge University Press, 1975.

068.   Power, Eileen. "The Education of Women." In M. M. Posten, ed., *Medieval Women*, pp. 76-88. Cambridge: Cambridge University Press, 1975.

069.   ———. *Medieval English Nunneries.* Cambridge, England: The University Press, 1922.

070.   Radcliffe-Umstead, Douglas, ed. *The Roles and Images of Women in the Middle Ages and Renaissance.* Pittsburgh: Center for Medieval and Renaissance Studies, 1975.

071.   Shank, Michael H. "A Female University Student in Late Medieval Kraków." *Signs: Journal of Women in Culture and Society 12* (1987): 373-380.

072.   Stuard, Susan M., ed. *Women and Medieval Society.* Philadelphia: University of Pennsylvania Press, 1976.

The Renaissance

073.   Bell, Susan Groag. "Christine de Pizan (1364-1430): Humanism and the Problem of a Studious Woman." *Feminist Studies 3* (1976): 173-184.

074.   Brink, J. R. *Female Scholars: A Tradition of Learned Women Before 1800.* Montreal: Eden Press Women's Publications, 1980.

075.   Chojnacki, Stanley. "Patrician Women in Early Renaissance Venice." *Studies in the Renaissance 21* (1974): 176-203.

076.   Gabriel, Astrik L. "The Educational Ideas of Christine de Pisan." *Journal of the History of Ideas 16* (1955): 3-22.

077.   Gibson, Joan. "Educating for Silence: Renaissance Women
        and the Language Arts." *Signs: Journal of Women in
        Culture and Society 14* (1989): 9-27.

078.   Gundersheimer, Werner L. "Women, Learning, and Power:
        Eleonora of Aragon and the Court of Ferrara." In
        Patricia H. Labalme, ed., *Beyond Their Sex: Learned
        Women of the European Past*, pp. 43-65. New York: New
        York University Press, 1980.

079.   Holm, Janice Butler. "The Myth of a Feminist Humanism:
        Thomas Salter's 'The Mirrhor of Modestie'." *Soundings
        67* (1985): 443-452.

080.   Hull, Suzanne W. *Chaste, Silent, and Obedient: English Books
        for Women, 1475-1640*. San Marino: Huntington Library,
        1980.

        Jardine, Lisa. (see 008).

081.   Kelly-Gadol, Joan. "Did Women Have a Renaissance?" In
        Women, History and Theory, pp. 19-50. Chicago:
        University of Chicago Press, 1984.

082.   Kelly, Joan. "Early Feminist Theory and the *Querelle des
        Femmes*, 1440-1789." In *Women, History, and Theory*, pp.
        65-108. Chicago: University of Chicago Press, 1984.

083.   Kelso, Ruth. *Doctrine for the Lady of the Renaissance*. Urbana,
        IL: University of Illinois Press, 1956.

084.   King, Margaret L. "Book-Lined Cells: Women and Humanism
        in the Early Italian Renaissance." In Patricia H.
        Labalme, ed., *Beyond Their Sex: Learned Women of the
        European Past*, pp. 66-90. New York: New York
        University Press, 1980.

085.   Kristeller, Paul Oskar. "Learned Women of Early Modern
        Italy: Humanists and University Students." In Patricia
        H. Labalme, ed., *Beyond Their Sex: Learned Women of
        the European Past*, pp. 91-116. New York: New York
        University Press, 1980.

086.   Labalme, Patricia H. "Women's Roles in Early Modern
        Venice: An Exceptional Case." In *Beyond Their Sex:
        Learned Women of the European Past*, pp. 129-152. New
        York: New York University Press, 1980.

087.   McLeod, E. *The Order of the Rose: The Life and Ideas of
        Christine de Pisan*. London: Chatto and Windus, 1978.

088.   Norman, Marion. "A Woman for All Seasons: Mary Ward
        (1585-1645), Renaissance Pioneer of Women's Education."
        Paedogogica Historica 23 (1983): 125-143.

089.   Ong, Walter. "Latin Language Study as a Renaissance
        Puberty Rite." *Studies in Philology 56* (1959): 103-124.

090.   Sachs, Hannelore. *The Renaissance Woman*. New York:
        McGraw-Hill, 1971.

091.   Simon, Joan. *Education and Society in Tudor England*.
        Cambridge, England: Cambridge University Press, 1966.

092.   Woodward, William Harrison. *Studies in Education During
        the Age of the Renaissance, 1400-1600*. New York:
        Teachers College Press, 1967.

The Reformation

093.   Bainton, Roland H. *Women of the Reformation in Germany
        and Italy*. Boston: Beacon Press, 1971.

094.   ————. *Women of the Reformation in France and England*.
        Boston: Beacon Press, 1973.

095.   ————. "Learned Women in the Europe of the Sixteenth
        Century." In Patricia H. Labalme, ed., *Beyond Their Sex:
        Learned Women of the European Past*, pp. 117-128. New
        York: New York University Press, 1980.

096.   Balmuth, Miriam. "Trends in Female Schooling and Literacy:
        England, 1500-1700." Paper presented at the 18th
        Annual Conference of the New York State Reading
        Association, Kiamesha Lake, New York, November 7,
        1984. ERIC: ED 264 149.

097.   Fraser, Antonia. *The Weaker Vessel*. New York: Vintage
        Books, 1985.

098.   Green, Lowell. "The Education of Women in the
        Reformation." *History of Education Quarterly 19* (1979):
        93-116.

099.   Marshall, Sherrin, ed. *Women in Reformation and Counter-
        Reformation Europe: Private and Public Worlds*.
        Bloomington, IN: University of Indiana Press, 1989.

100.   Monter, E. William. "Women in Calvinist Geneva (1550-
        1800)." *Signs: Journal of Women in Culture and Society 6*
        (1980): 189-209.

The Enlightenment

101.   Bodek, Evelyn Gordon. "Salonières and Bluestockings:
        Educated Obsolescence and Germinating Feminism."
        Feminist Studies 3 (1976): 185-199.

102.   Goldsmith, Peter L. "Ambivalence Towards Women's
        Education in the Eighteenth Century: The Thoughts of
        Dr. Vicesimus Knox II." *Paedogogica Historica 19* (1979):
        315-327.

103.   Johnson, R. Brimley, ed. *Bluestocking Letters*. London: John
        Lane, 1926.

104.   Lougee, Carolyn C. "Noblesse, Domesticity, and Social
        Reform: The Education of Girls by Fénelon and
        Saint-Cyr." *History of Education Quarterly 14* (1974):
        87-113.

105.   Mason, Amelia Gere. *Women of the French Salons*. New York:
        Century Co., 1891.

106.   Reynolds, Myra. *The Learned Lady in England, 1650-1750*.
        Glouster, MA: Peter Smith, 1964.

107.   Russell, Rosalind. "Elizabeth Hamilton: Enlightenment
        Educator." *Scottish Educational Review 18* (1986): 23-30.

108. Scott, Walter S. *The Bluestocking Ladies*. London: John Greene and Co., 1947.

109. Silver, Catherine Bodard. "Salón, Foyer, Bureau: Women and the Professions in France." In Mary Hartman and Lois W. Banner, eds., *Clio's Consciousness Raised*, pp. 72-85. New York: Octagon Books, 1974.

110. Spencer, Samia. "Women and Education." In *French Women and the Age of Enlightenment*, pp. 83-96. Bloomington: Indiana University Press, 1984.

Some Early European Plans for the Education of Women

111. Ascham, Roger. *Works*. London: J. R. Smith, 1865.

112. Bruni, Leonardo. "Du Studiis et Literis." Trans., H. W. Woodward. In *Vittorino de Feltre and Other Humanist Educators*. New York: Columbia University Teachers College, 1963.

113. Bruto, Giovanni Michele. *The Necessarie, Fit and Convenient Education of a Young Gentlewoman*. London and Amsterdam, 1598.

114. Courtney, Luther Weeks. *Hannah More's Interest In Education and Government*. Iowa City: Iowa University Press, 1925.

115. DeMolen, Richard L., ed. *Richard Mulcaster's Positions. Classics in Education, No. 44*. New York: Teachers College Press, 1971.

116. Gabriel, Astrik L. *The Educational Ideas of Vincent of Beauvais*. Notre Dame, IN: University of Notre Dame Press, 1956.

117. Jones, M. C. *Hannah More*. Cambridge: Cambridge University Press, 1952.

118. Kaufman, Gloria. "Juan Luis Vives on the Education of Women." *Signs: Journal of Women in Culture and Society 3* (1978): 891-896.

119. More, Hannah. *Strictures on the Modern System of Female
      Education.* London: T. Cadell, Jr. and W. Davies, 1799.

120. Plato. *The Republic* (esp. Ch. 5). Trans., G. M. A. Grube.
      Indianapolis: Hackett Publishing Co., 1974.

121. Rousseau, Jean Jacques. *The Emile* (esp. Ch. 5). Trans.,
      Allan Bloom. New York: Basic Books, 1979.

122. Saint Jerome. *Selected Letters.* Loeb Classical Library.
      London: Putnam and Co., 1933.

123. Tobin, Rosemary Barton. *Vincent of Beauvais' "De Eruditione
      Filiorum Nobilium": The Education of Women.* New
      York: Peter Lang, 1984.

124. Vegio, Maffeo. *De Educatione Liberorum, Book III*, Sections 2
      and 3. Basel: 1540.

125. Vives, Juan Luis. *Instruction of a Christian Woman: A Plan of
      Studies for Girls and the Duties of Husbands.* Trans.,
      Foster Watson. London: Longmans, Green and Co., 1912.

126. Watson, Foster, ed. *Vives and the Renaissance Education of
      Women.* New York: Longmans, Green and Co., 1912.

127. ———. *English Writers on Education, 1480-1603.* Gainesville:
      Scholars' Facsimiles and Reprints, 1967.

128. Wollstonecraft, Mary. *A Vindication of the Rights of Women.*
      Edited by Carol H. Poston. New York: W. W. Norton,
      1975.

129. Woodward, William Harrison. *Vittorino da Feltre and Other
      Humanist Educators.* New York: Teachers College Press,
      1963.

130. ———. *Desiderius Erasmus Concerning the Aims and Methods
      of Education.* Cambridge, England: University Press,
      1904.

CHAPTER 2

Themes in Women's Education in the United States

I began to reflect upon life rather seriously. . . .
What was I here for? What could I make of Myself? Must
I submit to be carried along with the current, and do just
what everybody else did? No: I knew I should not do that,
for there was a certain Myself who was always starting up
with her own original plan or aspiration before me, and
who was quite indifferent as to what people generally
thought.

—*Lucy Larcom*

It should not be surprising that the largely European colonists who settled in what was to become the United States brought with them their internalized ideas of women's role, women's place, and women's education. Thus, European themes in the education of women are also largely observable when one looks at the education of women in the United States. However, although the themes are present, both their relative importance and their actual expression differ, sometimes significantly.

The purpose of this chapter is to briefly outline the influence of the new world and the particular political and social realities of a new country on women's education, and to trace, generally, the nature of that education as it expanded—in concert with major social and institutional change in the United States—from fundamental illiteracy, confinement to the private sphere, and an emphasis on "household arts," to a not-uncommon college education, a move into the public sphere, and the lack of much instruction in homemaking at all. In a sense, the effort is to see what became of European beliefs and practices with respect to the education of women as both the beliefs and the women were increasingly transformed. Again, these themes are in no way intended to be all-encompassing of women's educational experience. Rather, they represent one way of framing questions about the education of women and one way of providing comparative information.

The bibliography for this chapter is a general one, and is intended to provide a background in the history of women's experience in the United States, with some attention to several general works on women's educational history over time. For the most part, works on specific aspects of women's education in the

35

United States, in specific periods, are grouped in following chapters
according to the purposes they address.

Attitudes Toward Women's Education: The Role of Religion, Politics, and Science

Negative attitudes toward the education of women continued in
the colonial period and thereafter; indeed, they exist today. However,
they have in some degree been mediated, combined with other themes
in women's education, submerged and masked by several important
factors, notably Protestant religion, republican politics, and the
increasing importance of science and technology.

The Role of Religion

One example of the mediation of religion on negative attitudes
toward the education of girls can be found in the religious ethos of
early Puritan settlers in New England. Included in that ethos was a
strong belief in salvation through knowledge of and adherence to
Biblical scripture. In order to ensure such salvation for all its
children, the Massachusetts Bay theocracy placed an emphasis on the
ability to read. Thus, although education for the role of wife, mother,
and homemaker continued to be the basis of most instruction for girls,
some kind of literacy instruction was also included. This did not,
however, often include instruction in the ability to write, for writing
was deemed largely unnecessary for women.

A second example of the way in which religion mediated
negative attitudes can be found in the story of the Protestant
religious revival movements of the early 19th century, which fueled a
hundred-and-fifty-year-old trend toward an alliance between the
Protestant minister and the white, middle-class woman. As
industrialization encouraged the employment of men in settings away
from home and increasingly separated the lives of men and women
into different spheres, many men ceased to attend church, leaving
congregations largely constituted of women and children. Association
with churches offered women both the limitations of relegation to
private life and the chance to gain experience in the (public) work of
the church, which was considered an appropriate extension of the
home for women's activities. As Nancy Cott notes, women "flocked
into churches and church-related organizations. . . . Women's prayer
groups, charitable institutions, missionary and education societies,
Sabbath School organizations, and moral reform and maternal
associations all multiplied phenomenally after 1800, and all of these
had religious motives" (144, p. 141). Both the values and the skills

learned in working for the church formed an important part of the foundation for rebellion and reform in the latter half of the 19th century.

Political Ideas in the New Republic

The influence of republican politics in a new and experimental democracy also mediated negative attitudes toward the education of girls and women. During and after the Revolutionary period, and well into the 19th century, political and educational policy makers shared the belief that a new republic required a particular, and particularly political, kind of education for its citizens. Since not many individuals of either sex went to school for very long, this consideration, in part, led to the conclusion that mothers had a special and important role to play in the education of both their sons and daughters. The notion of the importance of the "republican mother" thus mediated the notion that women didn't need any education apart from that required for domestic tasks. They did need, it was argued, enough formal education to enable them to be suitable teachers to their families. Although there are some who argue that the inclusion of girls in the common school of the 19th century was a natural outgrowth of the attendance of girls at dame schools and other proprietary or "adventure" schools (see, for example, Tyack and Hansot, 172), the public argument for such inclusion was based largely on the perceived need for mothers as early teachers who would raise the future generations of young republicans. In either case, the common school further extended access of girls to formal education and set the stage for women to become teachers of the young in actual schools. It is interesting to note that this argument for the important part played by mothers as teachers is very close to that extended by early Protestants in Germany during the Reformation: in both cases, the desire to promote a new institution—one religious and the other political—overcame the notion that women were intellectually inferior to men.

The Role of Science in Women's Education

By the latter half of the 19th century, a third factor emerged as important in shaping attitudes toward the education of women: the development of new technology and the growth of science as a way of understanding the world. Two examples may illustrate the ways in which these factors worked to increase the access of women to formal education, to prepare them for their role as homemakers in a more technological home, and, at the same time, to mask deeply-held prejudices against their education. First, the technical aspects of housekeeping changed during the 19th century. Many products formerly made at home, including cloth, soap, and preserved food became consumer items made by someone else, usually in a factory of some kind. At the same time, technology introduced mechanical devices to aid the housewife in her daily tasks—the vacuum cleaner and the washing machine are two important examples of late 19th century home appliances. On one hand, these changes offered some women—usually middle class, white women—some free time to pursue other interests served by education. One thinks of the development of community libraries, for example, which were frequently founded and run by women volunteers. At the same time, the education of girls changed to include not how to produce items for household use and how to compare them so as to get the most value for their money but how to use them. In an important sense, the education of girls for future roles as homemakers became an education in consumerism.

The growth of science as a (often **the**) way of knowing had a variety of effects on women's education. Catharine Beecher, for example, spent the better part of her life establishing female seminaries that included science in the curriculum. Her argument was that if women were to achieve equal status with men, albeit in their own sphere, they must understand the scientific basis on which their homemaking was predicated. Thus, it was insufficient for women to know how to cook and preserve food; they must also understand the chemistry of food preparation and preservation. It was largely through her efforts, and work of several other early proponents of women's education, that young girls in the United States achieved access to higher education at all.

At the same time, some men used knowledge emerging from the new interest in science in an effort to prevent women from gaining access to traditional higher, or college, educations. Dr. Edward Clarke (136), for example, wrote an extremely influential book in 1873, in which he expounded the notion that "subjecting" women to the stresses and strains that higher education would place on their intellect would deflect physical energy away from their bodies, causing their reproductive organs to shrink, thus making them unable to bear children. Offered as an objective conclusion derived from scientific inquiry, this theory gained wide notoriety and acceptance.

Similarly, the work of the educational psychologists G. Stanley Hall and Edward Thorndike utilized new scientific ideas to promote both separate and unequal education for women (170). Hall, a student of Freud, Jung, and Darwin, idealized women as saviors of civilization. He also believed that women were lower on the evolutionary scale than men, often appearing, as the social conventions of the day demanded, both more emotional and less rational. He was unalterably opposed to coeducation, and, indeed, to any advanced eduction for women, writing that "it is utterly impossible to hold girls to the same standards of conduct, regularity, severe moral accountability, and strenuous mental work that boys need" (170, p. 367). Rather, he thought, after the age of 12 they should be educated separately through a curriculum directed toward motherhood (170, p. 368). Even when girls were educated in coeducational schools, their curriculum should be designed around non-intellectual education. Thorndike, although 30 years younger than Hall, and considerably more liberal, believed that although males and females had the same *average* intelligence, there was more *variability* in the intelligence of males than in the intelligence of females. Thus, a greater number of males would have intelligence rated at the upper end of the scale. In consequence, although girls could and should be educated for such roles as teachers, nurses, librarians, and social workers, which demanded average intelligence, they clearly were unsuited either for leadership in these fields or for the more "intellectual" professions (170, pp. 369-370). Both Hall and Thorndike believed that heredity was more important than environment in human behavior, and they shared the belief that males and females inherited different traits. Thorndike identified the fighting instinct for men and the nursing instinct for women as inherent in male and female heredity, clearly following widely accepted social conventions for sex role differentiation. Thus, the belief that women were intellectually inferior, if not inherently evil, was masked by adherence to scientific theory, which, in turn, gave rise to "scientific" study and corroborating results.

It can be said with some justification that although negative attitudes toward the education of women in the United States were mediated by a variety of factors, and that women in the United States achieved early access to some levels of formal education, those same attitudes ensured that their access to higher education and to intellectually demanding professions was considerably delayed and often prevented altogether until well into the 20th century. Ironically, while the role of the mother as educator was elevated to public status in the United States, and while religious ideas and collaboration with established churches helped to give women extensive educational experience in community activism, their very identification with that status served to reinforce their exclusion from an education that would give them the knowledge that was most valued in the society, particularly scientific knowledge.

Women's Access to Formal Education

In many ways, the history of women's education in the United States has been a story of gradually but irrevocably increasing access to higher and higher forms of schooling. Private female academies were founded as early as the late 18th century, and the emergence of the common elementary school in the 1830s and 1840s carried girls into school in large numbers. Although the struggle to establish female seminaries on an academic par with boys' academies was a long one, it was accomplished by the end of the Civil War and the fight to create both the social climate and the means for girls' high school and college education was won by the beginning of the 20th century.

In other ways, however, the story is neither so simple nor so sanguine. For one thing, like their counterparts in Europe, women in the United States were educationally divided by social class. Millions of girls in the 19th century received little formal schooling, and went, instead, to work on farms and in cotton mills and other industries. Until the advent of the child labor laws at the end of the century, girls (and boys) whose parents needed their economic or physical help simply did not send them to school. Similarly, but more tragically, black girls (and boys) were prohibited by law in some states even from learning to read and write, and it was only through the efforts of some determined black (and white) women (and men) after the Civil War that public schooling for black children began to become a reality.

It is true that, like their contemporaries in Europe, a few women claimed an education beyond the basics. For the most part, these were upper-class white women who had the time and the books to read for themselves. Many of these women, particularly in the first half of the 19th century, remained unmarried, partly by choice but also because they were deemed to be unacceptable as marriage partners because of their erudition. These women, however, were exceptions to the rule. In general, the "learned woman" or "bluestocking" as she was often called, was not an ideal type of woman in the United States. Such women did, however, provide incalculable services to later generations of women. Judith Sargent Murray, who wrote some of the most cogent arguments for the inclusion of girls in the common school, Susan B. Anthony, who led the fight for women's suffrage, and Jane Addams, who founded the social settlement movement, all were highly educated women who devoted their lives not to a particular family but to the human one.

In the 20th century, the battle regarding women's formal education has taken place on several fronts. One is the struggle to open the professions to women. In the first half of the century, women gained entry into nursing, social work, librarianship, and other professions which became associated with "women's work." The barriers in medicine and law have fallen in just the past twenty-five years, but entry and retention in engineering, architecture, and the physical sciences still lags behind. A second front is the analysis of the actual educational experiences of girls in schools. While boys and girls today are routinely treated to the same school conditions, the same teachers, the same curricula, and the same educational activities, qualitative differences exist in educational outcomes for females. Teachers and guidance counselors are still speaking with the culture's tongue, still discouraging girls from taking advanced courses in math and science, and still enculturating girls for traditional roles as wives, mothers, and homemakers (162). A third front is the effort to create educational equity among different class, race, and ethnic groups, as well as for persons with disabilities. While these efforts are made on behalf of both boys and girls, some educators and policy makers are beginning to be concerned with a focus on the females in those groups.

While it is largely the case that women in the United States have achieved access to all levels of formal schooling, and, indeed, are for the first time the majority of college students, equity in all of these settings still eludes them. Females are still disproportionately majoring in literature, history, the romance languages, and the professions traditionally associated with women—teaching, nursing, and social work. Female instructors at the high school and college level are fewer in number than males, and at the college level are less likely to be full professors. Similarly, women are less likely to be leading theorists in any discipline. Even in the field of medicine, women are disproportionately in the ranks of pediatricians and general practitioners rather than surgeons. It is difficult to measure whether these findings are a matter of personal choice or institutional bias. In part, both factors are probably operative. Nevertheless, the search for equity in schooling for women is not over.

The Extension of Motherhood to the Community

The theme of mothers as important teachers has been an important one in the United States, one that has gone beyond women's "traditional" role and carried the values of that role into community and national social life. Not only have real mothers been considered teachers in the home, women as both real and symbolic mothers have been at the forefront of social change for all of our history.

At first, skills acquired to take care of families were extended to neighbors. Women were early midwives, for example, and practiced that profession in both agrarian and urban communities in both the north and south. Women were also the chief growers and mixers of herbal medicines, a skill they shared with family and community. They were also often the members of the community who sought help for less fortunate members, who took care of the mentally unstable, and who made room for orphaned children.

In the early decades of the 19th century, women entered public life in a major way by largely replacing men as teachers in the new common schools of the nation. What is particularly interesting about this movement is the rationale on which it was predicated by male policy makers. As the schoolmaster left the schoolhouse for better paying work in factory or business, and as public schools proliferated, there was an intense need for teachers. Young women, it was felt, were the perfect choice. Not only would they work for about one-third the salary of men, they also *were more naturally suited to dealing with young children by virtue of their role and education as women.* Thus, work in the common school, which was a school for young children, became an available avenue for extended opportunities for women outside of the home.

Experience (and further formal education) as teachers, in turn, frequently led to a more sophisticated view of the world. The "schoolmarm" often taught in towns distant from her own home. Indeed, after the Civil War, New England women went south in droves to teach in Freedmen's Schools, and many a young girl satisfied her desire for adventure or a better life by moving west and opening one-room schoolhouses on the prairie and in the mountains. While a majority of these women later married and were forced to stop teaching, some dedicated their lives to the occupation and others, like Catharine Beecher and Emma Willard, went on to create academies and colleges for women with curricula that matched those for men.

As women gained increasing access to higher education in the latter half of the 19th century, they began to look for ways to put their education to use, apart from homemaking. In concert with the Progressive movement at the end of the century, women increasingly took their "mother" role into the public world in variety of reform movements. Spurred on in many cases by participation in the abolitionist movement prior to the Civil War, and through association with the women's rights movement that began in 1848, social feminists of various political beliefs argued with justification that an unregulated industrial economy created tragic and inhuman conditions for lower-class workers and immigrants. Whether the cause was abolition, or temperance, or urban and industrial reform, the notion that sent women into the south, the saloons, and the slums was the idea that the moral and intellectual knowledge gained through an education for and practice of motherhood could alleviate deplorable conditions for other human beings.

As women extended "motherhood" into public life, they gained invaluable educations in the ways of political and economic organizations that not only stood them in good stead in the fight for suffrage, but also gave them some of the tools to effect genuine societal reform. Indeed, it is difficult to overestimate the importance of that kind of education for 19th century women. It was of a kind not to be found anywhere else, and it served many of them well.

When the Progressive period had run its course, about the end of the 1920s, women found their influence shrinking once more from a national level to the level of home and community. But those women who, having helped to support their families during the Depression, and populate defense plants during World War II, now found themselves living in single family homes in the suburbs, were essentially different women from their great-grandmothers. They were, as a whole, better educated; they had had successful and important experiences in public life; and they were ready for Betty Friedan's naming of the "feminine mystique" (281). They were ready to reexamine the role of mother as a model, not only for education but for the world.

Women's Experience as an Educational Model

In the hundred and twenty years from 1848 to 1968, women's education—at home, at school, and in the political and economic trenches—had given them a new sense of power. Central to that sense was, first, a desire for equal rights—in business, in politics, in the arts, in short, in every area where men were currently in charge. As time passed, however, there reemerged the idea that the experience of women should not only be known, understood, and appreciated, but that it should become a viable model for social life. Nowhere was this more apparent than in education.

The development of women's studies as an area of inquiry in higher education gave impetus to women and men in a variety of disciplines to use women's experience as a lens through which history could be reinterpreted. With respect to education generally, scholars began to ask questions about who had been educated, where that education occurred, what the content of that education was, what limits there were on that education, and what results that education had produced. With respect to women's education, they asked the same questions, but also discovered long-forgotten stories of women who had made a difference—in education and in other fields as well.

Against this backdrop, feminists in professional education began to study the effects of gender on both historical and contemporary schooling and to consider possibilities for change in the content of our curricula, the way we interact with students, and the nature of our pedagogy. What emerged was a model of education quite different from traditional models. Where traditional models focus on competition, feminist models focus on cooperation; where traditional models focus on sorting, labeling and exclusion, feminist models focus on inclusion; where traditional models focus on academic subjects, feminist models focus on people; where traditional models focus on individuality and separation, feminist models focus on connection. Beyond that, some feminists in education began to question the very definition of the "educated" person (801), arguing that without the incorporation of women's educational experiences, the traditional picture of educational history and philosophy is incomplete and therefore inaccurate.

Central to the contribution of women's studies scholars in education has been an interest in moral education (785, 802) that asks both how schooling and other forms of education can become more moral and how it can produce a more moral society. At the heart of these questions is the old/new idea that the role of motherhood may be the source of important ideas for educational theory and practice.

As women have done periodically throughout history, these scholars formed groups—in this case based on professional associations—to support one another and to serve as vehicles for public policy debate. The National Women's Studies Association, the National Council for Research on Women, the Special Interest Group/Research on Women in Education of the American Educational Research Association, the American Association of University Women, Girls' Clubs of America, and a number of discipline-based women's caucuses and organizations all work to further research, scholarship, and the making of public policy related to this model of education.

The success of these efforts has been mixed. On one hand, a body of rigorous scholarship now exists on which to base further study and recommendations. Similarly, curricula that incorporate women's experience have been developed at all levels of schooling. On the other hand, gender has not become a matter of national public policy debate regarding schooling and although studies of educational outcomes now often distinguish by gender in their reporting, the education of girls is not a matter of significant concern in schools or in teacher education programs.

Nevertheless, the use of women's experience as a model of education is gaining adherents, sometimes under different rubrics. Much of the work in multicultural education, for example, incorporates ideas that are also found in feminist models. Indeed, it may well be that the future effectiveness of these models may lie in the degree to which they can be useful in developing a more sophisticated way of understanding many forms of human diversity. Whatever the case, it is clear that the story of women's education in the United States is not over. There is a long way to go; we are perhaps half-way there.

BIBLIOGRAPHY

General Background Works

131. Beard, Mary R. *America Through Women's Eyes*. New York: Greenwood Press Reprint, 1969.

132. Berkin, Carol and Norton, Mary Beth, eds. *Women of America: A History*. Boston: Houghton Mifflin, 1979.

133. Boothe, Viva B. *Women in the Modern World*. Philadelphia: The American Academy of Political and Social Science, 1929. (Reprinted, 1974, by Arno Press).

134. Buhle, Mari Jo, Gordon, Ann G., and Schrom, Nancy. "Women in American Society: An Historical Contribution." *Radical America 5* (1971): 3-66.

135. Chafe, William. *The American Woman: Her Changing Social, Economic and Political Roles, 1920-1970*. New York: Oxford University Press, 1970.

136. Clarke, Edward D. *Sex in Education*. Boston: Osgood, 1874.

137. Conway, Jill K. *The Female Experience in Eighteenth- and Nineteenth-Century America: A Guide to the History of American Women*. New York: Garland, 1982.

138. Cott, Nancy F. *Root of Bitterness: Documents of the Social History of American Women*. New York: E. P. Dutton, 1972.

139.   ———. *The Bonds of Womanhood: "Woman's Sphere" in New England, 1780-1935*. New Haven: Yale University Press, 1977.

140.   ———. and Pleck, Elizabeth, eds. *A Heritage of Her Own: Toward a New Social History of American Women*. New York: Simon and Schuster, 1979.

141.   Demos, John. *Entertaining Satan: Witchcraft and the Culture of Early New England*. New York: Oxford University Press, 1982.

142.   de Tocqueville, Alexis. *Democracy in America*, ed. Phillips Bradley. New York: Vintage Books, 1954.

143.   Edwards, Lee R. and Diamond, Arlyn. *American Voices, American Women*. New York: Avon Books, 1973.

144.   Friedman, Jean E., and Shade, William G., eds. *Our American Sisters: Women in American Life and Thought, 2nd rev. ed.* Boston: Allyn and Bacon, 1976.

145.   Gorham, Deborah. *The Victorian Girl and the Feminine Ideal*. Bloomington: Indiana University Press, 1982.

146.   Hall, G. Stanley. *Adolescence*. New York: D. Appleton, 1907.

147.   Hartman, Mary and Banner, Lois W., eds. *Clio's Consciousness Raised*. New York: Harper Torchbooks, 1974.

148.   Hymowitz, Carol and Weissman, Michaele. *A History of Women in America*. New York: Bantam Books, 1978.

149.   James, Edward T., ed. *Notable American Women, 1607-1950*, 3 vols. Cambridge, MA: Belknap Press, Harvard University Press, 1971.

150.   Kava, Beth Millstein and Bodin, Jeanne, eds. *We, the American Women: A Documentary History*. Chicago: SRA, 1983. (Revised ed.)

151. Kelley, Mary, ed. *Woman's Being, Woman's Place: Female Identity and Vocation in American History.* Boston: G. K. Hall, 1979.

152. Kerber, Linda K. and Matthews, Jane DeHart, eds. *Women's America: Refocusing the Past.* New York: Oxford University Press, 1982.

153. ———. *Women of the Republic: Intellect and Ideology in Revolutionary America.* New York: W. W. Norton, 1986.

154. Koehler, Lyle. *A Search for Power: The "Weaker Sex" in Seventeenth Century New England.* Urbana, IL: 1980.

155. Lerner, Gerda. *The Majority Finds Its Past.* New York: Oxford University Press, 1979.

156. Lifton, Robert Jay, ed. *The Woman in America.* Boston: Beacon Press, 1986.

157. Riley, Glenda. *Inventing the American Woman: A Perspective on Women's History, 1607-1877.* Arlington Heights, IL: Harland Davidson, 1986.

158. ———. *Inventing the American Woman: A Perspective of Women's History, 1865 to Present.* Arlington Heights, IL: Harland Davidson, 1986.

159. Ryan, Mary P. *Womanhood in America from Colonial Times to the Present.* New York: 1975.

160. Scott, Anne Firor. *The Southern Lady: From Pedestal to Politics, 1830-1930.* Chicago: University of Chicago Press, 1970.

161. ———. *The American Woman: Who Was She?* Englewood Cliffs, NJ: Prentice-Hall, 1971.

General Works on Education

162. Chapman, Anne. *The Difference It Makes: A Resource Book on Gender for Educators.* Boston: National Association of Independent Schools, 1988.

163. Clifford, Geraldine Joncich. "Saints, Sinners, and People: A Position Paper on the Historiography of American Education." *History of Education Quarterly 15* (1975): 257-272.

164. Faragher, John M. and Howe, Florence, eds. *Women and Higher Education in American History.* New York: W. W. Norton, 1988.

165. Goodsell, Willystine. *The Education of Women: Its Social Background and Its Problems.* New York: Macmillan, 1924.

166. Hansot, Elizabeth and David Tyack. "Gender in American Public Schools: Thinking Institutionally." *Signs: Journal of Women in Culture and Society 13* (1988): 741-760.

167. Howe, Florence, ed. *Myths of Coeducation—Selected Essays.* Bloomington, IN: Indiana University Press, 1984.

168. Rury, John. "Imagining Gender in Educational History: Themes from Lives of Colonial Women." *Educational Foundations 2* (1988): 45-60.

169. Schwager, Sally. "Educating Women in America." *Signs: Journal of Women in Culture and Society 12* (1987): 333-372.

170. Seller, Maxine. "G. Stanley Hall and Edward Thorndike on the Education of Women: Theory and Policy in the Progressive Era." *Educational Studies 11* (1981): 365-374.

171. Sexton, Patricia. *Women in Education.* Bloomington, IN: Phi Delta Kappa, 1976.

172. Tyack, David and Hansot, Elisabeth. *Learning Together: A History of Coeducation in American Schools.* New York: The Russell Sage Foundation, 1990.

173. Woody, Thomas. *A History of Women's Education in the United States,* 2 vols. New York: Science Press, 1929.

PART II

EDUCATING WOMEN FOR A PURPOSE

PART II

EDUCATING WOMEN FOR A PURPOSE

*The great aim of education is not knowledge, but
action.*

—Herbert Spencer

Introduction

While the term *education* has many definitions and is linked to
a variety of activities (for example, the processes of enculturation,
socialization, development, instruction, and training), it is always the
case that education is purposeful and has both intended and
unintended outcomes (174). Indeed, the education of women may
provide the clearest of all examples of that dictum, because with the
exception of the few women of the upper classes who aspired to and
acquired a classical education, instruction for girls and women has
been primarily directed toward specific, often immediate ends. Many
boys, on the other hand, especially boys of the middle and upper
classes in the United States, have had access to the kind of formal
education in the liberal arts, sciences, and classics which has a more
indirect purpose and outcome. Girls were taught to "do" something;
boys were taught to think about what could be done.

An examination of the purposes of women's education can
expand the study of education in several ways. First, because so
much of the education of girls has been "informal," it can raise
questions about the comparable "informal" education of boys—for
example, about instruction in farming and in craft and semi-
professional occupations, which for most of history has been
accomplished through apprenticeship systems. Second, because so
much of women's education has been circumscribed by their social
class and their roles as wives and mothers within a particular social
class structure, it can raise questions about the specific socialization
practices of a variety of institutions that enculturate boys and girls to
their social class and masculine roles, which is a subject that is
widely ignored in the study of education. Third, because historically
the education of boys and girls has not been coterminous, a study of
the purposes of women's education can provide alternative
interpretations of educational history more generally (081, 168) and
can make a significant contribution to the study of the history of
education as a social enterprise.

For these reasons, this section of the book has been organized
in terms of four general purposes or outcomes of women's education:
education for hearth and home, education for paid work, education for
civic responsibility and action, and the development of higher
education for women. The historical thread in these sections is not
linear, that is, each section does not discuss a period that precedes the
next. Rather, an attempt has been made to examine each type of
purpose from the Colonial period to the 20th century. In addition, it
is well to keep in mind that, in part because the education of girls
was largely outside the confines of schools, it was often
multidimensional as well. Thus, there is not always a clear
distinction between, for example, education for hearth and home and
education for civic responsibility. Indeed, the socialization of girls as
caretakers and the instruction of girls in caretaking skills has been
an important foundation for their roles in providing "care" for the
larger community and for their induction into such "caregiving"
occupations as teaching, nursing, social work and the operation and
maintenance of offices.

Similarly, the outcomes of women's education were often of
greater variety than the outcomes of the education of men. Perhaps
another way to say this is that women's education has had more
unintended outcomes. Thus, for example, the inclusion of girls as
participants in the common school in the 19th century was not
intended to lead to their role as school teachers, nor to the
development of higher education for women, nor to their significant
social contributions as political rebels or cultural reformers. That
such outcomes occurred can be attributed, in part, to an inclination on
the part of male policy makers to think of women only in terms of
their role in the home. No one, apparently, thought through the
possible consequences of formal education for girls until after the
middle of the 19th century, and then it was too late. Although formal
schooling for girls continued to be spoken of in terms of its relation to
their "female" roles, the women who benefitted from that schooling
continued to put it to other uses.

BIBLIOGRAPHY

174.   Lichter, Hope Jensen. "Families and Communities as
        Educators: Some Concepts of Relationship." In *Families
        and Communities as Educators*, pp. 3-94. New York:
        Teachers College Press, 1979.

CHAPTER 3

Education for Hearth and Home

A woman who is skilled in every useful art, who practices every domestic virtue . . . may, by her precept and example, inspire her brothers, her husband, or her sons, with such a love of virtue, such just ideas of the true value of civil liberty . . . that future heroes and statesmen, who arrive at the summit of military or political fame, shall exultingly declare, it is to my mother I owe this elevation.

—Miss P. W. Jackson, on graduating from Mrs. Rowson's Academy

The Colonial Wife

The lives of women in the American colonial period were often hard, beset by sadness and loss, and short. In the first colonies in Virginia, the death rate was high, women married very early and those who did not die in childbirth often were widowed several times. Marriage was longer lasting and more stable in New England due, in part, to a better climate, but babies there (as in the south) were frequently lost to disease, work was neverending, and the religious ethos was often harsh. In the vast majority of cases, both in the north and in the south, education for girls consisted of education for the role of wife, mistress of the household, and mother.

For those who look for inequity in the lives of women and men, both in terms of daily life and in terms of education, there is much to be found. Marriage and family were the predominant future perceived for young girls and married women were denied by law the inheritance of property, the right to buy and sell land without their husbands' permission, and the right to go to town schools. In New England, the illiteracy rate among women was higher than it was among men, although this may be misleading because literacy rates are often traced by looking at signings of wills and other legal documents, and girls were often taught to read but not to write. The intellectual "nature" of women was thought to be significantly less able than that of men and thus they were "naturally" less needful of formal education.

At the same time, it would be a mistake to think that girls and women received no education at all; indeed, their education was deliberate, precise, and extensive. It consisted primarily of learning how to manage a household, rear children, and be in other ways a good wife.

The skills necessary for success in these endeavors were not simple matters in the early days of colonial life. Although sometimes aided by relatives and servants, mistresses of households in both New England and the Southern colonies were responsible for every aspect of household life, including producing cloth and sewing it into clothing; the growth, processing, cooking and preserving of food; the growth and judicious application of herbal and other medicines; acting as midwives for family and neighbors; cleaning the house and its furnishings; taking care of livestock; and bearing, raising, and teaching the children. In addition, the wife often kept the household accounts, served as a partner in family business enterprises, and, certainly after the beginning of the 19th century, was held to be responsible for the moral development of her husband and children, if not the entire community.

In general, women acquired the knowledge and skills they needed in the same way as men, through apprenticeships with family elders or with community members in their own towns or elsewhere. Indeed, it was not unusual for families to send daughters to live with other families as indentured servants. Brownlee and Brownlee (302) include in their work several examples of indenture contracts which indicate that a variety of particular household skills were to be taught to the young women involved. Not infrequently, reading was among those skills.

Emphasis on literacy varied over the colonial period and depended to a large extent on which of the colonies one lived in and to the prevailing religious beliefs and practices. In New England, Puritan beliefs regarding salvation influenced parents to teach all their children to read so that they could understand the Bible. In the middle colonies, there appears to have been a more equitable attitude toward the education of girls. Quaker families, for example, were more likely to view males and females as equal in the sight of God; certainly there was always the provision for women speaking in meetings and assuming leadership roles in the community (349). Quakers in the middle colonies built and maintained elementary schools for both boys and girls long before their contemporaries in New England, and women often served as speakers in the church. Similarly, German, Moravian, and Dutch Reformed settlers were early proponents of elementary education for all their children. In the southern colonies, women were in such short supply that their

early experiences differed substantially from their sisters in the
north. Because they were often considerably younger than their
husbands, and because of their sparse numbers, they were likely to
marry more than once. Thus, they were frequently granted more
legal rights to inherit property. With the advent of slavery, some
were likely to have help with the more onerous household tasks, and
were able to devote themselves to spinning, weaving, embroidery and
other artistic needlework as well as to gardening. The system of
formal education in the south also differed from that of the north; the
population was more spread out, towns were not as readily accessible,
and the wealthier families established a system of tutorial education
for their children in which live-in tutors were often part of the family
entourage. In this situation, girls sometimes were taught along with
their brothers, and sometimes given educational attention when the
boys were otherwise occupied.

If women did not share legal equality with men in the colonial
years, it can be said that they were equally as important in their
contributions to the maintenance of home, family and community.
Indeed, in some respects their very importance as homemakers may
have prevented them from taking advantage of any access they may
have had to formal schooling, both because of the time needed for
household tasks and because men felt that encouraging their
education might very well lead to their "forgetting" their duties at
home.

Nevertheless, there were well educated women in the colonies,
both in the north and south. It is here that issues of class as well as
region again become important in understanding the total educational
situation for women. Some upper-class girls, especially those whose
fathers felt some interest in educating daughters as well as sons,
achieved considerable learning, often under the tutelage of fathers
but also through their own efforts. Women whose names may be
somewhat familiar to us today—Anne Bradstreet, Anne Hutchinson,
Mercy Warren, Elizabeth Ferguson, Deborah Logan, Susanna Wright
and Hannah Griffiths—were all women of learning, some of whom
paid a terrible price for their education. Anne Hutchinson, for
example, was driven from the Massachusetts Bay Colony in disgrace
for daring to teach Bible lessons to other women.

As the 18th century progressed, more and more girls were sent
to school, first to dame schools run by women in their homes, and
then, if their families were willing and could afford it, to proprietary
or "adventure" schools. Although the quality of the dame school
varied widely from place to place, as an institution it provided some
form of child care for colonial families and helped to prepare boys for
admittance to the higher grammar schools, which girls could not

attend, and to offer girls basic literacy skills in the alphabet and in
ciphering, and to prepare them in rudimentary housekeeping skills.
For those girls whose parents could afford to send them on to private
"venture" schools which taught music, dancing, embroidery, French
and other subjects designed to make girls more marriageable, the
dame school also provided a basis for further education.

Public education for girls was longer in coming than for boys,
especially in the New England states. Although families in the
middle states did provide public education for both boys and girls, in
New England girls had to be "smuggled in" (172, p. 13). Girls often
attended classes taught by the local schoolmaster early in the
morning or late in the afternoon, after the boys were gone. As time
went on, girls increasingly were taught in summer sessions, when
boys were needed elsewhere. Hansot and Tyack argue that these
"summer schools" provided the historical basis for the coeducational
common school that emerged in the 1830s and 1840s in the United
States (172) because they served to show that girls could, indeed,
learn like their brothers. In matters of schooling, however, as in
other educational activities, the prevailing idea was that girls should
be educated for their lives in the home; if schooling was good for girls
it was good because it made them better wives, mothers, and
homemakers, not because it opened literary or intellectual doors to
them.

By the latter part of the 18th century, as the colonies were
gearing for war and independence, literacy rates among men and
women in all sections of the country were about equal. The
Revolution, however, created in the minds of many a new role for
women and stimulated a significant change in attitudes toward
women's formal education. After 1776, the colonial wife became,
more than anything, the republican mother.

The Republican Mother

The role of the mother as teacher reached perhaps its zenith in
the notion of the republican mother in the early part of the 19th
century. Following independence, the young country was faced with
the task not only of formulating a government and creating a viable
economy, but also of raising future generations to understand their
responsibilities in maintaining a democratic society governed not by a
hereditary elite but by the people. This latter task was assigned to
women, who were told from the pulpit, the newspaper, and the
popular journal that the success or failure of the American
experiment rested on their shoulders.

What happened in the years between 1776 and 1840 was not that women moved from the private sphere of the family to the public sphere of commerce. Indeed, the division between public and private, which had been relatively blurred in the colonies, was established in earnest in the early 19th century. Rather, the private role of women in the family was given a public responsibility. As Kerber notes, the role of women was to be both domestic and political (153, p. vi). No longer were women to be simply competent homemakers; now they needed in addition the kind of knowledge that would enable them to raise their sons for independent thought and participation in republican government. No longer were women perceived as only moral instructors; now they were to be political instructors as well. No longer were the daughters of wealthy families to be schooled to become passive but graceful additions to their husbands' lives; now they were to become self-reliant, confident, and above all, rational.

This, of course, necessitated a new conception of women's intellectual abilities. As long as women's intellect was perceived to be inferior to men's, it was hard to argue for their public role as initial teachers to a nation. There emerged, therefore, a strong argument for women's access to schooling best articulated, perhaps, by Judith Sargent Murray and Benjamin Rush, who both focused on the need to educate women away from dependence and toward the new ideal of the republican mother. Reform proposals for the education of girls proliferated, although most did not go so far as to promote the education of girls to the same level as boys. Rather, girls were to receive a solid elementary education with their brothers, in female academies and in the new common school. Rush's proposal for educating girls included "reading, grammar, penmanship, 'figures and bookkeeping,' geography, the first principles of natural philosophy [science], vocal music (because it soothed cares and was good for the lungs) but not instrumental music (because, except for the most talented, it seemed a waste of valuable time), and history (as an antidote to novel reading)" (211, pp. 45-46).

It is important to remember that the ability to go to school was not ever perceived as a prelude to higher learning. Indeed, the "learned woman" was in as much disrepute as ever for higher learning was thought to ruin a woman for useful life. Rather, what was needed was a stronger, more literate, knowledgeable and moral mother. This emphasis on an ideal mother became, by the middle of the 19th century, what Welter has called the "cult of true womanhood" (271).

The "True" Woman

The "true" woman of the middle of the 19th century was a predominantly middle-class white woman bound to the home in the service not only of the family and the state, but of the church. Central to the emergence of the "true" woman were the changes brought about by the industrial revolution which, in a sense, actually created the separation of public and private spheres by literally separating families: fathers left home and cottage industry to work in factories and business; mothers remained at home to care for children. It also, of course, helped to enlarge the middle class to significant proportions and to create a substantial working class that encompassed laboring women who could never, by definition, achieve "true" woman status because they could not stay at home.

A second major factor in the growth of the ideal of the "true" woman was a growing and symbiotic relationship between the middle-class woman and the Protestant church. During the first half of the 19th century, male membership in organized churches declined and women became instrumental as congregants and workers in the church. Pastors, who in colonial times had been persons of high status and exercised political influence, increasingly lost their central position in society and it was to women that they turned for support and allegiance. Sermons were increasingly directed toward women and their roles as wives and mothers and women became idealized as the moral center of the society. Nor did women disappoint them. Rather, they assumed wide-ranging responsibilities in church affairs and in the process began to move their roles in the home out into the community.

Religion was a powerful force not only in legitimizing the public activities of many women, but also in setting the standards of morality and behavior which became a template for the development of women's "character." It is safe to say that without their roles in church activities—missions, congregational duties, and Bible study groups, as well as in the social reform movements that characterized much of the 19th century—women in the United States would have had a much harder time gaining the educational experiences that led them to demand access to higher education. Indeed, some have said that without the notion of the "true" woman, access to formal education beyond elementary school or female academy might never have been possible (168).

Yet the cult of the true woman placed enormous restrictions on the middle-class wife. The old puritan love-affair with sin reemerged during the industrial expansion, but in a new guise. Sin, it was argued, existed "out there," in the dirt and grime of the factory where greedy men engaged in unregulated competition for economic gain. The home, on the other hand, existed to provide a safe haven of moral rectitude—and a social balance of good vs. evil in the society. Women, of course, now better educated and situated as the "mothers of the republic," were the arbiters of that domain.

The "cult of true womanhood" consisted of four related ideas. First, there was a sharp distinction between home and the economic world that paralleled a perceived distinction between male and female nature. Second, the home was designated as the female's only sphere of influence. Third, women were considered morally superior to men. And finally, the role of the mother was idealized in terms of her attention to and sacrifice for husband and children (254, p. 33). This ideal was taught vociferously not only from the pulpit, but also in schoolbooks and by an enormous collection of mass publications— women's magazines, pamphlets on how to raise daughters, religious tracts, and other periodicals. It may be said that the role of 19th-century public and popular media had a great deal to do with the education of girls in that period—perhaps more than schooling or any other form of educational activity (267). For the education of the "true" woman was, in large part, a psychological education. Harris, for example, has noted that the difference between the Puritan and Victorian periods lay in the source of women's repression. For the Puritan, repression was external; for the Victorian, it was internal (254, p. 51).

Some scholars have pointed out (244, 271) that during this period middle-class white women traded power in the home for power in the marketplace. At the same time, the ideal of the "true" woman was opposed to conceptions of women's intellectual capacity that had been widely promoted only a few decades earlier. Indeed, as women became more in possession of an elementary education, and more powerful in the home, beliefs about their ability to achieve academic and intellectual heights declined. Domestic repetitive tasks were seen as "helping" women "overcome" the stresses of their biological nature. As Harris notes, it was believed by many that "shocks, unfeminine activities, and intellectual pursuits [would rob] their uteri of adequate supplies of blood and energy" (254, pp. 40-41).

The paragon of the "true" woman was, in many respects, an ideal unrealized in practice. Certainly, this notion was at odds with the lives of working-class women who labored in factories and shops to help support their families. Nor did it reflect the lives of black women, either slave or free, who struggled against nearly insurmountable odds on a daily basis just to make ends meet. But it was a powerful notion nonetheless and affected lower-class women in somewhat cruel ways. If the ideal woman were one who managed her

home, extended comfort to husband, children, and the poor, and
sought to create a moral balance to a wicked world, all the while
struggling against a weak physical makeup and an inferior
intellectual capacity, then those who did not have the luxury to stay
at home and emulate the model were somehow lesser creatures, often
in their own eyes as well as in the eyes of the public. Nor was this
image of comfort to those women who did not marry. Deprived of
their central function as women, they were often completely
dependent upon relatives for support and lacked standing in the
community. The spinster—one who has nothing to do but
spin—became not only a relatively useless person, but the object of
ridicule as well.

Still, this period saw important advances in women's academic
instruction, from dame school to common school to female seminary.
Such education was not perceived as terribly threatening to the
established order, since it was, in all respects, designed to provide
education for hearth and home. In many ways, it simply did not
"count" as "real" education at all, that is, education for public life.

The "Modern" Housewife

An important aspect of the "true" woman was a shift in her
responsibilities from producer to consumer that has continued to this
day. Education for the tasks of running a household changed from
instruction in how to grow, process, and manufacture household needs
to instruction in how to select and use a variety of products and
appliances, and for the middle-class woman, how to manage servants
of various kinds or deal with trade and craftspeople.

Although the woman of the 19th century was still largely
responsible for the production of medicines and cosmetics, by the end
of the Civil War new knowledge had begun to make inroads in these
responsibilities, both in medicine and in other fields. An enormous
influx of cheap labor that came to the United States, starting with
the Irish potato famine in the 1840s and swelling to the millions
toward the end of the century created a situation in which middle-
class women could have "help" with the housework. In addition,
many families sent daughters into the teaching force in the common
schools, saw them off to the west on the great expansion movement,
and sent them to school in the new high schools that emerged during
the latter half of the century. If the "true" woman stayed at home
and managed her household, the "new" woman was more inclined to
be on her way somewhere else. As will be shown in a later section,
many of these "new" women went to college.

The question then arose, How will our young girls learn to fulfil their primary responsibilities as homemakers? In part, this question was more sound than substance. In truth, most girls still learned their homemaking lessons at home. But many did not. By the beginning of the Progressive movement around the 1880s, urban young women were taking sewing and cooking classes in public school. These classes were the female equivalent of manual training for boys, a movement which began to emerge at that time. Initially designed as something of an afterthought—why would homemaking need to become a subject in school?—these classes foreshadowed the development of the home economics movement that probably reached its apex in the first two decades of the 20th century (590).

The argument for the study of home economics rested, finally, on a renewed argument for increasing the skills of girls for their future role as homemakers. As young women increasingly stayed in school longer and then went into a variety of occupations, concern was raised about their ability to manage homes, which was, of course, their "real" occupation. The answer, according to Rury (590), was the incorporation of home economics in the schools as the female equivalent of industrial education for boys. As its name implies, home economics shifted the role of homemaker from a political one (the republican mother) to an economic one (an efficient mother). Moreover, the steady advance of technology for the home encouraged supporters to argue that homemaking was becoming more complex, and that formal instruction was needed to prepare young women for an "industrial" home. "Tomorrow," said Ellen Richards, one of the founders of home economics, in 1911, "the woman who is to be really mistress of her house must be an engineer, so far as to be able to understand the use of machines, and to believe what she is told" (590, p. 26).

The most compelling argument, however, was an echo of the earlier argument for elementary schooling for girls. Then, the country needed sons who could govern themselves; now the country needed sons who were well organized, obedient, and healthy workers. What better place could be found to instill these values than the home, and who better to foster them than the mother in that home?

The belief that instruction in domestic science, or home economics, would, in fact, improve the home and strengthen the family rested on an assumption that industrial principals of efficiency would work in the home. Such was not often the case. Nevertheless, while such instruction never became the universal core of women's education as its founders had hoped, it did become an important part of women's education for the home, as did the establishment of the Girl Scouts and girls' clubs of various kinds. Indeed, it can probably

be said that as the 20th century unfolded, more education for the
home has been provided by nonschool and nonhome agencies than by
either teachers or mothers, although, ironically, the public view of
their importance as homemakers has not abated.

Indeed, one of the interesting things about studying the
education of girls for homemaking is to note how little there is of it
today. It is not unusual, for example, for girls to leave home without
knowing how to cook food from scratch, how to clean thoroughly as
their mothers and grandmothers did, or how to take care of young
children. At the end of the 20th century, with nearly 70% of mothers
of young children in the workforce and with the proliferation of
convenience food and household services, the education of girls for
hearth and home has become largely the property of girls' clubs, mass
media magazines, newspaper columnists like Heloise, cookbook
authors and publishers, child psychologists and pediatricians who
write developmental manuals for young mothers, home economics
departments of utility companies, food processors and distributors,
and television "home" programs and talk shows. Clearly, other
interests and occupations have come to occupy a central place in
women's education.

BIBLIOGRAPHY

The Colonial Wife

175. Auwers, Linda. *The Social Meaning of Female Literacy:
        Windsor, Connecticut, 1660-1775*. Chicago: Newberry
        Library Papers in Family and Community History, No.
        77-4A.

176. ———. "Reading the Marks of the Past: Exploring Female
        Literacy in Colonial Windsor, Connecticut." *Historical
        Methods, XIII* (1980): 204-214.

177. Axtell, James. *The School Upon a Hill: Education and Society
        in Colonial New England*, Ch. 5. New York: W. W.
        Norton, 1976.

178. Demos, John. *A Little Commonwealth: Family Life in
        Plymouth Colony*. New York: Oxford University Press,
        1970.

179. Dunn, Mary Maples. "Saints and Sisters: Congregational and Quaker Women in the Early Colonial Period." In Janet Wilson James, ed., *Women in American Religion*, pp. 27-46. Philadelphia: University of Pennsylvania Press, 1978.

180. Gilmore, William. "Elementary Literacy on the Eve of the Industrial Revolution: Trends in Rural New England, 1760-1830." *Proceedings of the American Antiquarian Society 92* (1982): 114-126.

181. Hiner, N. Ray. "The Cry of Sodom Enquired Into: Educational Analysis in Seventeenth-Century New England." *History of Education Quarterly 13* (1973): 3-22.

182. Johnson, James. "The Covenant Idea and the Puritan View of Marriage." *Journal of the History of Ideas 32* (1971): 107-118.

183. Keller, Rosemary Skinner. "New England Women: Ideology and Experience in First-Generation Puritanism." In Rosemary Radford Ruether and Rosemary Skinner Keller, eds., *Women and Religion in America, Vol. 2*, pp. 132-192. New York: Harper and Row, 1983.

184. Lockridge, Kenneth. *Literacy in Colonial New England: An Enquiry into the Social Context of Literacy in the Early Modern West.* New York: W. W. Norton, 1974.

185. Long, Huey B. *Continuing Education of Adults in Colonial America.* Syracuse, NY: Syracuse University Publications in Continuing Education, 1973.

186. Lyons, C. H. "The Colonial Mentality: Assessment of the Intelligence of Blacks and Women in Nineteenth Century America." In P. G. Altbach and G. P. Kelly, eds., *Education and Colonialism.* New York: Longman, 1978.

187. Martin, George H. "The Early Education of Girls in Massachusetts." *Education 20* (1900): 323-327.

188. Monaghan, E. Jennifer. "Literacy Instruction and Gender in Colonial New England." *American Quarterly 40* (1988): 18-41.

189.   Moran, Gerald F. "'Sisters' in Christ: Women and the Church
       in Seventeenth-Century New England." In Janet Wilson
       James, ed., *Women in American Religion*, pp. 47-65.
       Philadelphia: University of Pennsylvania Press, 1978.

190.   —— and Maris A. Vinovskis. "The Puritan Family and
       Religion: A Critical Appraisal." *William and Mary
       Quarterly 39* (1982): 29-49.

191.   ——. "The Great Care of Godly Parents: Early Childhood
       in Puritan New England." In Alice B. Smuts and John
       W. Hagen, eds., *History and Research in Child
       Development* (Monographs of the Society for Research in
       Child Development, vol. 50, nos. 4-5). Chicago:
       University of Chicago Press, 1986.

192.   Morgan, Edmund. *The Puritan Family*. New York: Harper
       and Row, 1966.

193.   Norton, Mary Beth. "The Evolution of White Women's
       Experience in Early America." *Journal of American
       History 89* (1984): 593-619.

194.   Seybolt, Robert F. *The Private Schools of Colonial Boston*.
       Cambridge: Harvard University Press, 1935.

195.   Sklar, Kathryn Kish. "Growing Up Female in Eighteenth-
       Century Massachusetts." Paper delivered at the
       University of Michigan, 1977.

196.   Small, Walter H. "Girls in Colonial New England." *Education
       22* (1902).

197.   ——. *Early New England Schools*. Boston: Ginn, 1914.

198.   Spruill, Julia. *Women's Life and Work in the Southern
       Colonies*, Chs. 11-14. New York: W. W. Norton, 1972.

199.   Ulrich, Laurel Thatcher. "Vertuous Women Found: New
       England Ministerial Literature, 1668-1735." In Janet
       Wilson James, ed., *Women in American Religion*, pp. 67-
       87. Philadelphia: University of Pennsylvania Press, 1978.

200.   ——. *Good Wives: Image and Reality in the Lives of Women in Northern New England, 1650-1750*, Part One. New York: Oxford University Press, 1980.

201.   Vinovskis, Maris A. "Family and Schooling in Colonial and Nineteenth-Century America." Paper presented at Conference on the Family in Historical Perspective, Clark University, Worcester, Massachusetts, November 14-16, 1985.

The Republican Mother

202.   Alcott, Bronson. *Observations on the Principles and Methods of Infant Instruction*. Boston: Carter and Hendee, 1830.

203.   Bailey, Ebenezer, ed. *The Young Ladies' Class Book: A Selection of Lessons for Reading in Prose and Verse*. Boston: 1831.

204.   Clinton, Catherine. "Equally Their Due: The Education of the Planter Daughter in the Early Republic." *Journal of the Early Republic 2* (1982): 39-60.

205.   Clio. "Thoughts on Female Education." *Royal American Magazine* (1774): 9-10.

206.   Eastman, Mary. "The Education of Women in the Eastern States." In Annie Nathan Meyer, ed., *Woman's Work in America*, pp. 3-53. New York, 1891.

207.   Green, Nancy. "Female Education and School Competition, 1820-1850." *History of Education Quarterly 18* (1978): 129-142.

208.   Humphrey, Herman. *Domestic Education*. c. 1840.

209.   James, Janet Wilson. *Changing Ideas about Women in the United States, 1776-1825*. New York: Garland Publishing, 1981.

210.   Keller, Rosemary Skinner. "Women, Civil Religion, and the American Revolution." In Rosemary Radford Ruether and Rosemary Skinner Keller, eds., *Women and Religion*

in America, Vol. 2, pp. 368-408. New York: Harper and Row, 1983.

211.   Kerber, Linda. "Daughters of Columbia: Educating Women for the Republic, 1787-1805." In Stanley Elkins and Eric McKitrick, eds., *The Hofstader Aegis: A Memorial*, pp. 36-59. New York: Alfred A. Knopf, 1974.

212.   ———. "The Republican Mother: Women and the Enlightenment—An American Perspective." *American Quarterly 28* (1976): 187-205.

213.   ———. "The Republican Ideology of the Revolutionary Generation." *American Quarterly 38* (1985): 462-488.

214.   ———. "Why Should Girls Be Learned or Wise?" In *Women of the Republic*, pp. 185-231. New York: W. W. Norton, 1986.

215.   ———. "We Own That Ladies Sometimes Read." In *Women of the Republic*, pp. 233-264. New York: W. W. Norton, 1986.

216.   Kuhn, Anne L. *The Mother's Role in Childhood Education: New England Concepts, 1830-60*. New Haven: Yale University Press, 1947.

217.   Macauley, Catharine. *Letters on Education with Observations on Religious and Metaphysical Subjects*. London: C. Dilly, 1790.

218.   MacLear, Martha. *The History of the Education of Girls in New York and New England, 1800-1870*. Washington, DC: Howard University Press, 1926.

219.   Mann, Horace. *A Few Thoughts on the Powers and Duties of Woman*. Syracuse: Hall, Mills, 1853.

220.   Murray, Judith Sargent. "On the Equality of the Sexes." *The Massachusetts Magazine* (March 1790): 132-135.

221.   ———. *The Gleaner*. Boston, 1798.

222.   Norton, Mary Beth. "Eighteenth-Century American Women in
        Peace and War: The Case of the Loyalists." *William and
        Mary Quarterly 33* (1976): 386-409.

223.   ———. *Liberty's Daughters: The Revolutionary Experience of
        American Women—1759-1800*, Ch. 9. Boston: Little,
        Brown, 1980.

224.   Riley, Glenda. "Origins of the Argument for Improved Female
        Education." *History of Education Quarterly 9* (1969):
        455-470.

225.   Rush, Benjamin. *Thoughts Upon Female Education,
        Accommodated to the Present State of Society, Manners,
        and Government in the United States of America*
        (Philadelphia and Boston, 1787). Reprinted in Frederick
        Rudolph, ed., *Essays on Education in the Early Republic*
        (Cambridge, MA: 1865).

226.   Schultz, Stanley K. *The Culture Factory: Boston Public
        Schools, 1789-1860*. New York: Oxford University Press,·
        1973.

227.   Tyack, David. "The Common School and American Society: A
        Reappraisal." *History of Education Quarterly 26* (1986):
        301-306.

228.   Tyler, Alice Felt. "The Education of a New England Girl in
        the Eighteen-Twenties." *New England Quarterly 17*
        (1944).

229.   Wilson, Joan Hoff. "The Illusion of Change: Women and the
        American Revolution." In Alfred F. Young, ed., *The
        American Revolution: Explorations in the History of
        American Radicalism*, pp. 385-445. DeKalb, IL: Northern
        Illinois University Press, 1976.

The "True" Woman

230.   Alaya, Flavia. "Victorian Science and the 'Genius' of
        Women." *Journal of the History of Ideas 38* (1977): 261-
        280.

231.   Alcott, Louisa May. *Little Women*. New York: Collier Books,
        1962.

232.   Bacon, Martha. "Miss Beecher in Hell." *American Heritage 14*
        (1962): 28-31, 102-105.

233.   Beecher, Catharine. *Suggestions Respecting Improvements in
        Education, Presented to the Trustees of the Hartford
        Female Seminary and Published at Their Request.*
        Hartford: Packard and Butler, 1829.

234.   ——. *A Treatise on Domestic Economy, for the Use of Young
        Ladies at Home, and at School*. Boston: Marsh, Capen,
        Lyon, and Webb, 1841.

235.   ——. *Letters to Persons Who Are Engaged in Domestic
        Service*. New York: Leavitt and Trow, 1842.

236.   ——. *The Evils Suffered by American Women and American
        Children: The Causes and the Remedy*. New York:
        Harper and Row, 1846.

237.   ——. *Woman's Profession as Mother and Educator, with
        Views in Opposition to Woman Suffrage*. Boston: G.
        Maclean, 1872.

238.   ——. "The Peculiar Responsibilities of American Women." In
        Nancy F. Cott, ed., *Root of Bitterness*, pp. 171-177. New
        York: E. P. Dutton, 1972.

239.   Bloch, Ruth H. "American Feminine Ideas in Transition: The
        Rise of the Moral Mother, 1785-1815." *Feminist Studies 4*
        (1978).

240.   Boylan, Anne M. "Growing Up Female in Young America,
        1800-1860." In Joseph M. Hawes and N. Ray Hiner, eds.,
        *American Childhood: A Research Guide and Historical
        Handbook*, pp. 153-184. Greenwich, CT: Greenwood
        Press, 1985.

241.   Branch, Edward Douglas. *The Sentimental Years, 1836-1860*.
        New York: D. Appleton-Century Co., 1934.

242. Brenzel, Barbara. "Domestication as Reform: A Study of the Socialization of Wayward Girls, 1856-1905." *Harvard Educational Review 50* (1980): 196-213.

243. ———. *Daughters of the State: A Social Portrait of the First Reform School for Girls in North America, 1856-1905.* Cambridge, MA: MIT Press, 1983.

244. Bunkle, Phillida. "Sentimental Womanhood and Domestic Education, 1830-1870." *History of Education Quarterly 14* (1974): 13-30.

245. Burstyn, Joan N. "Catharine Beecher and the Education of American Women." *New England Quarterly 47* (1974): 386-403.

246. ———. *Victorian Education and the Ideal of Womanhood.* London: Croom Helm, 1980.

247. Bushnell, Horace. *Christian Nurture.* New York: C. Scribner, 1861.

248. Conway, Jill K. "Stereotypes of Femininity in a Theory of Sexual Evolution." In Martha Vicinus, ed., *Suffer and Be Still: Women in the Victorian Age,* pp. 140-154. Bloomington: Indiana University Press, 1973.

249. Cott, Nancy F. "Young Women in the Second Great Awakening in New England." *Feminist Studies 3* (1975): 15-29.

250. Degler, Carl. "What Ought to Be and What Was: Women's Sexuality in the Nineteenth Century." *American Historical Review 79* (1974): 1467-90.

251. Douglas, Ann. *The Feminization of American Culture.* New York: Alfred A. Knopf, 1977.

252. George, Margaret. "From 'Goodwife' to 'Mistress': The Transformation of the Female in Bourgeois Culture." *Science and Society 37* (1973): 157-159.

253.   Hale, Sarah Josepha. *Manners; or, Happy Homes and Good Society All the Year Round.* Boston: J. E. Tilton and Co., 1868.

254.   Harris, Barbara J. "The Cult of Domesticity." In *Beyond Her Sphere: Women and the Professions in American History,* pp. 32-72. Westport, CT: Greenwood Press, 1978.

255.   Harveson, Mae Elizabeth. *Catharine Esther Beecher: Pioneer Educator.* Philadelphia: The Science Press, 1932.

256.   Kelley, Mary. "The Sentimentalists: Promise and Betrayal in the Home." *Signs: Journal of Women in Culture and Society 4* (1979): 434-436.

257.   Lacey, Barbara E. "Women and the Great Awakening in Connecticut" (Ph.D. diss., Clark University), 1982.

258.   Lasch, Christopher and Taylor, William R. "Two Kindred Spirits: Sorority and Family in New England, 1839-1848." *New England Quarterly 36* (1963): 23-41.

259.   Legates, Marlene. "The Cult of True Womanhood in Eighteenth-Century Thought." *Eighteenth Century Studies 10* (1976): 21-39.

260.   Parker, Gail. "Mary Baker Eddy and Sentimental Womanhood." *New England Quarterly 53* (1970): 3-18.

261.   Perkins, Linda. "Black Women and Racial 'Uplift' Prior to Emancipation." In Filomina Chioma Steady, ed., *The Black Woman Cross-Culturally.* Cambridge, MA: Schenkman, 1981.

262.   ———. "The Impact of the 'Cult of True Womanhood' on the Education of Black Women." *Journal of Social Issues 39* (1983): 17-28.

263.   Ryan, Mary P. *The Empire of the Mother: American Writing about Domesticity, 1830-1860.* Binghamton, NY: Haworth Press, 1982.

264.   Sklar, Kathryn Kish. *Catharine Beecher: A Study in American Domesticity.* New Haven: Yale University Press, 1973.

265. Smith-Rosenberg, Carroll and Rosenberg, Charles. "The Female Animal: Medical and Biological Views of Women in Nineteenth Century America." *Journal of American History 60* (1973): 332-56.

266. Smith-Rosenberg, Carroll. "The Hysterical Woman: Some Reflections on Sex Roles and Role Conflict in 19th Century America." *Social Research 39* (1972): 652-678.

267. Thompson, Eleanor Wolf. *Education for Ladies: 1830-1860: Ideas on Education in Magazines for Women.* New York: King's Crown Press, 1947.

268. Vicinus, Martha, ed. *Suffer and Be Still: Women in the Victorian Age.* Bloomington: University of Indiana Press, 1973.

269. Walters, Ronald G., ed. *Primers for Prudery.* Englewood Cliffs, NJ: Prentice-Hall, 1974.

270. Weisberger, Bernard A. *They Gathered at the River: The Story of the Great Revivalists and Their Impact on Religion in America.* Boston: Little, Brown, 1958.

271. Welter, Barbara. "The Cult of True Womanhood." *American Quarterly 18* (1966): 151-174.

272. ———. "Anti-Intellectualism and the American Woman, 1800-1860." *American Quarterly 28* (1976): 151-174.

273. ———. *Dimity Convictions: The American Woman in the Nineteenth Century.* Athens, OH: Ohio University Press, 1976.

274. ———. "The Feminization of Religion." In *Dimity Convictions: The American Woman in the Nineteenth Century*, pp. 83-102. Athens, OH: Ohio University Press, 1976.

275. ———. "She Hath Done What She Could: Protestant Women's Missionary Careers in Nineteenth-Century America." *American Quarterly 30* (1978): 624-638.

276. Zelizer, Viviana A. *Pricing the Priceless Child: The Changing Social Value of Children.* New York: Basic Books, 1985.

The "Modern" Housewife

277.   Baker, Elizabeth F. *Technology and Women's Work*. New
        York: Columbia University Press, 1964.

278.   Beck, Sarah. *The Gender Factor: The Apportionment of Work
        in American Households*. New York: Putnam, 1985.

279.   Bernard, Jessie. *Women, Wives, Mothers: Values and Options*.
        Chicago: Aldine, 1975.

280.   ———. *The Female World*. New York: The Free Press, 1981.

281.   Friedan, Betty. *The Feminine Mystique*. New York: Dell,
        1963.

282.   Gilbreath, Lillian M. *The Home-Maker and Her Job*. New
        York: D. Appleton and Co., 1927.

283.   Gilman, Charlotte Perkins. *Women and Economics: a Study of
        the Economic Relation Between Man and Woman as a
        Factor in Social Evolution*. Boston: Small, Maynard and
        Co., 1898.

284.   ———. *The Home, Its Work and Influence*. New York: McClure,
        Phillips, and Co., 1903.

285.   Hartmann, Heidi I. "The Family as the Locus of Gender,
        Class and Political Struggle: The Example of
        Housework." *Signs: Journal of Women in Culture and
        Society 6* (1981): 366-394.

286.   Kaledin, Eugenia. *Mothers and More: American Women in the
        Fifties*. Westport: Twayne Publishers, 1984.

287.   Komisar, Lucy. "The Image of Woman in Advertising." In
        Vivian Gornick and Barbara Moran, eds., *Women in
        Sexist Society: Studies in Power and Powerlessness*, pp.
        304-317. New York: Signet, 1972.

288.   Lake Placid Conferences on Home Economics. Proceedings of
        First through Tenth Annual Conferences. Lake Placid,
        NY: 1901-1908.

289. Laslett, Barbara. "The Family as a Public and Private Institution: An Historical Perspective." *Journal of Marriage and the Family 35* (1973): 480-492.

290. Laslett, Peter. "The Comparative History of the Household and the Family." *Journal of Social History 4* (1970): 75-87.

291. ———. *Household and Family in Past Time.* Cambridge, Eng.: Cambridge University Press, 1972.

292. Lerner, Gerda. "Just a Housewife." In *The Majority Finds Its Past*, pp. 129-144. New York: Oxford University Press, 1979.

293. Lucas, Bertha. *The Woman Who Spends: A Study of Her Economic Function.* Boston: Whitcomb and Barrows, 1904.

294. McGaw, Judith A. "Women and the History of American Technology." *Signs: Journal of Women in Culture and Society 7* (1982): 798-828.

295. Oakley, Ann. *Women's Work.* New York: Vintage Books, 1976.

296. O'Donnell, Lydia N. *The Unheralded Majority: Contemporary Women as Mothers.* Lexington, MA: Lexington Books, 1985.

297. Richards, Ellen H. "Ideal Housekeeping in the Twentieth Century." *Journal of Home Economics 3* (1911): 174-175.

298. "The Sexual Politics of Housework." *Utne Reader* (March-April 1990): 65-89.

CHAPTER 4

Education for Paid Work

*I would give my daughters every accomplishment
which I thought proper, and to crown all, I would early
accustom them to habits of industry and order. They
should be taught with precision the art economical; they
should be enabled to procure for themselves the
necessaries of life; independence should be placed within
their grasp.*

—*Judith Sargent Murray*

At the end of the 18th century when Judith Sargent Murray
wrote the words quoted above, she was arguing against an education
that would make girls life-long dependents on fathers and husbands
and for an education that would make them confident and self-reliant.
Those attributes, she thought, came when girls could support
themselves by working independently outside the home. Murray did
not envision the revolution of women in the workforce that was to
come; indeed, her idea of "working for pay" tended to focus on the
pursuit of such "womanly" occupations as needlework (349, p. 3).
Nevertheless, for a large number of white, middle- and working-class
girls, the first step taken on the road to such independence was when
they began to "keep school" as teachers of young children.

The Teaching Daughter

Jensen argues that in the years from 1790 to 1850, the United
States underwent a major shift with respect to attitudes about the
education of many of its women. In the early part of that period, the
argument in favor of women's education centered on their role as
republican mothers and teachers of their own children. By the 1820s,
"a second ideology was taking form, one that I would like to label 'the
ideology of the teaching daughters,' in which writers argued the
benefits of employing women as teachers" (349, p. 3).

Occurring in both New England and the mid-Atlantic states,
the movement of young women into schoolrooms resulted from several
societal factors. First, as the nation became more populated, more
and more schools were built and had to be staffed. With the advent of
the common school, which was designed to provide public education to

all (or most) children, there was a critical need for teachers. Second, girls were increasingly attending proprietary schools which taught basic literacy and a variety of ornamental subjects designed to produce a genteel young lady. Additionally, a number of female academies that offered a more advanced curriculum of study were founded in the early years of the 19th century by such women as Catharine Beecher, Emma Willard, and Mary Lyon. Girls who attended these schools had already had a good basic education and often desired to use it in some kind of professional way. Third, the marriage age of young women went up, leaving a kind of "window" of several years during which they needed something to do. Fourth, male schoolmasters, who sometimes only taught for a few years anyway, were leaving the profession of teaching to find work in other, better paying occupations. Fifth, and certainly not inconsequential, young women would work for about one-third the salary of men.

Initially, particularly in New England, girls entered teaching often little better prepared than their older students (336). They were often very young, sometimes only 16 or 17 years old, did not view teaching as a life-long occupation, usually were assigned to teach only the younger children, and hardly ever reached positions of authority over men, who were the principals and other school leaders. There is considerable evidence to suggest, however, that earning their own money, having a certain respected status in the community, and—perhaps more than anything else—being able to contribute to the education of others were powerful rewards for these first teachers (004, 378). Contradicting much of the accepted historical picture of the life of the "schoolmarm," letters and diaries of these teachers portray their excitement at "keeping school," as well as their determination to continue their own education for the benefit of their students.

Not all young women who went into teaching were simply the products of a common school education, however. Melder, for example, describes a variety of private experiments in educating teachers that existed at least twenty years before the first public normal school sponsored by Horace Mann opened its doors in 1839 (357). Emma Willard's Troy Female Academy sent 200 young women into teaching before that time and Catharine Beecher was an early advocate of education specifically designed for teachers from the 1820s on. Less well known but of equal importance, is the work of the Rev. Joseph Emerson and his students, Zilpah Grant and Mary Lyon, at the Ipswitch Seminary and the institution that was to become Mt. Holyoke College. While more about these schools will be said in a later section, here it can be asserted that each of these schools, and others as well, laid the groundwork for the professionalization of teaching that is once again at the forefront of educational debate today.

The "teaching daughters" of the 19th century were more than young women extending their "natural domestic duties" to the schoolhouse. They were also among the first identifiable groups of wage-earning women in the United States, particularly as they left their hometowns and spread out across the western reaches of the country. Through their efforts, and by their salaries, fathers were assisted in saving farms, older and younger brothers were sent on for higher education, and the women themselves were able to generate self-support when they needed to and achieve a degree of independence heretofore largely unknown to the middle-class girl. Indeed, although the prevailing social ideal of the woman whose function it was to sacrifice herself for a greater good caused some women to apologize for teaching specifically for money (354, p. 17), many young women who were without other means of support found in teaching the very means to survive. In the process, they created a profession for themselves, contributed to curricular and pedagogical advances for other women, and were a significant part of the movement to bring culture and civilization to the expanding republic.

The Laboring Woman

Lerner notes that in the colonial and revolutionary period, although most women worked in the home, they also served as "butchers, silversmiths, gunsmiths, upholsterers [and] ran mills, plantations, tan yards, shipyards, and every kind of shop, tavern, and boardinghouse; they were gate keepers, jail keepers, sextons, journalists, printers, 'doctoresses,' apothecaries, midwives, nurses, and teachers" (388, pp. 16-17). Thus, the notion of women "working for a living" is far from a new one in the history of the United States. Educational historians have provided some information on schooling for working-class girls, particularly with respect to vocational education. However, by defining education as schooling, they have neglected the role of education for paid work that has occurred outside of schools, and have therefore also seriously neglected the lower- or working-class girl as the subject of serious educational study.

Nevertheless, we do know something about the broader education of the laboring woman, particularly the white, largely farm women who worked first in the textile industry in New England and then in nearly all industries across the country; the black women, both slave and free, who worked on farms and plantations in the south and as domestics and, sometimes, in factories in the north; and the immigrant women who filled the sweatshops and other manufacturing industries in the latter half of the 19th and early 20th centuries.   Several societal factors link the experiences of laboring women—both native born and immigrant—in the 19th century. One of these is the increasing difference of their lives from those of their middle-class sisters (388), particularly in the urban northeast and midwest. In these areas, industrialization and specialization were more likely, and social class differences were more pronounced.

Industrialization also helped to create a second difference that links the experiences of laboring women, and that was both the nature and the source of education for women. For the middle-class girl, schooling and instruction in academic subjects became a principal source of education. For the lower-class girl, educational activities were more frequently sponsored by the workplace, by voluntary associations, and by social agencies and labor organizations. When lower-class girls did attend school, their curriculum diverged significantly from that of their white counterparts; for the poor girl, black or white, native or immigrant, vocational or industrial training often took the place of academic instruction. Formal schooling for these young women was specifically designed to be "useful," which meant useful in the home or useful in the workplace.

A third factor that links their experiences is the degree to which education received or obtained by laboring women was tied to domestic activities for hire or converted to mass production. That is, women of the working class most often found employment in shops and factories that focused on trades involving the manufacture of fabrics and sewing and the processing and selling of food, or in domestic service for people of a higher class.

In New England, perhaps the best example of this shift from home work to industrial work is the development of the cotton mills and the wholesale employment in those mills of young, unmarried or recently widowed, farm girls. These girls had a variety of reasons for coming to work in the mills. A contemporary account reveals some of them:

> One, who sits at my right hand at table is in the factory
> because she hates her mother-in-law. . . . The one next to
> her has a wealthy father, but like many of our country
> farmers he is very penurious, and he wishes his
> daughters to maintain themselves. . . . The next has a
> "well-off" mother, but she is very pious and will not buy
> her daughter so many pretty gowns and collars and
> ribbons . . . as she likes. . . . The next one has a horror of
> domestic service. The next one has left a good home

because her lover, who has gone on a whaling voyage,
wishes to be married when he returns, and she would
like more money than her father will give her (312, pp.
64-65).

The most famous of all the cotton mills were those established
in Lowell, Massachusetts by Frances Cabot Lowell, who brought the
power loom from the British Isles to the United States. Observing,
however, the miserable conditions in which British mill workers lived,
and often died, Lowell determined to create a system that would both
enhance profits and guarantee that Yankee farmers would allow their
daughters to work for him. He therefore established both the mills
and a series of institutions associated with them: boarding houses
directed by live-in matrons in which the mill girls were required to
live under strict guidelines; the practice of paying employees in
money rather than scrip (because, in many cases, the girls sent much
of their wages home); and a set of "educational" settings and
activities, including a library established by the company, lectures at
the Lyceum, a magazine which printed employee writing, and a
variety of other religious and cultural activities for employee benefit.
Lucy Larcom, perhaps the most famous of the "Lowell girls" because
of her detailed personal account (386, wrote:

We had all been fairly educated at public or private
schools, and many of us were resolutely bent on
obtaining a better education (306, p. 24).

Although the Lowell system appears benevolent, it is well to
remember that female employees worked 13-14 hours a day, six days
a week; had rigid curfews; performed repetitive tasks at fast-moving
machines; worked in crowded, poorly ventilated buildings full of
cotton fiber dust; and were paid significantly less than the men who
worked there (148, 306). They could be dismissed for "'immoral
conduct,' drinking, smoking, failure to attend public worship, lying,
'suspicious or bad character,' 'unauthorized absence,' 'boarding off the
corporation without leave,' expressing dissatisfaction over wages,
levity, hysteria, impudence, or simply not being liked by a particular
overseer" (306, p. 26). Nevertheless, they were better off than other
mill workers in southern New England and some of the middle states,
where the "English" system was often the rule. Still, women were
often among the labor leaders when exploitation eventually drove
mill workers to join together to protest and strike a number of mills.
Thus, while middle-class women were learning "public" skills in the

context of the church, lower-class women were learning some of those same skills in the context of a nascent labor movement.

Work by white farm girls in the New England cotton mills was to a large extent voluntary. This was not the case for black slaves in the south. There, black women worked on farms and plantations as both domestic "house" slaves, and field hands, often both at the same time. Not all slaves, however, worked in agricultural endeavors. Many worked in Southern cotton and textile mills, as well as in "turpentine camps, in sugar refineries, in food and tobacco processing, in rice mills, in foundries and saltworks, and in mines (where they pulled trams), and as lumberjacks, ditch diggers, and even construction workers, laying track for Southern railroads" (306, p. 99).

Subjected to potential and often very real forced separation from husbands and children, the continual threat of sexual imposition from white masters, and an overwhelming burden of physical work, black women nonetheless took advantage of what educational opportunities there were. House slaves, for example, were so much a part of plantation life and so low on the status scale that they were frequently "treated as nonexistent" (148, p. 42). Because this was so, however, "they were often able to use the information gathered in the big house to their own advantage and to the advantage of their fellow slaves" (148, p. 42). Although it was against the law to teach black children to read in the south, some white women did so. Similarly, literate black women living in Southern cities sometimes held secret schools for their own children and the children of others. Foner recounts the story of Susie King Taylor's "underground education":

> We went every day about nine o'clock with our books
> wrapped in paper to prevent the police or white persons
> from seeing them. We went in, one at a time, through
> the gate into the yard to the L kitchen, which was the
> school room. . . . After school we left the house the same
> way we entered, one by one (148, p. 104).

Free black women, in both north and south, normally worked to supplement the low pay of their husbands. In the north, most worked in domestic service, for industrial work was often barred to them. Black children in the north sometimes had access to formal schooling: the Quakers in Pennsylvania early provided schools for blacks and black churches were notable for their interest in schooling the children of their parishioners.

After the Civil War, black children in the south began to be allowed to go to school, separate though it was. The Freedmen's Bureau established a number of such schools, sometimes taught by white New England schoolteachers. Public schools in the south also were established, although black taxpayers had to support white schools before schools for their own children. Beyond elementary school, however, black boys and girls were most often sent to vocational schools that "offered their students narrow training designed to mold efficient workers rather than academic work intended to promote critical thinking skills and preparation for full citizenship" (385, p. 3). This emphasis on vocational education was also typical of schooling for the immigrant woman, who, like the black woman, suffered a double bind of prejudice: the former was female and foreign, the latter female and black. In either case, schooling was designed to maintain class boundaries and guarantee social control (391).

If the education of black women was limited, so, too, was the education of the immigrant woman. While some scholars maintain that immigrant aspirations for economic, communitarian, and civic advancement caused immigrant families to enthusiastically support their children's participation in the assimilation process of the public schools (392), others point out that large numbers of immigrant boys and girls were never able to take advantage of formal schooling, either because there was no room in the schools or because they had to go to work at an early age, or both (391).

Like black women, immigrant women were often considered "inferior" to white women. They were believed to be "dirty," lacking in knowledge of "proper" hygiene, and unable to maintain the healthy homes that would produce good workers. A major emphasis in the education of immigrant women, therefore, was home economics, designed to foster efficient homemaking according to middle-class standards. In this regard, Valli, in reviewing a collection of essays on education for women workers, makes an important distinction between "workers' education," and vocational education. In contrast to the latter, workers' education was "less formal than vocational education and broader in its structures and goals. It [was] a movement without formal degrees or institutional legitimation. Its students [were] not job seekers in need of work-related skills, but job holders eager to develop their social and cultural knowledge, their understanding of economic relations and conditions, and their leadership skills" (394, p. 44). Also in contrast to vocational education, which was supported by business, workers' education was affiliated with the labor movement.

Describing a long list of sources of education for immigrant women, Seller notes that the most determined providers of education were often the women themselves, aided at times by a variety of middle-class women's organizations (391). Among these were the

YWCA, settlement houses such as Hull House in Chicago and the Henry Street Settlement in New York, and both ethnic and mainstream churches. Parochial schools also played a significant role in educating the daughters of immigrant families. But for the most part, immigrant women cooperated in educating themselves, both in the culture of their home countries and of their adopted one, and the failure of public education to address the needs of intellectually gifted immigrant women is one of the sorriest aspects of the history of schooling in a presumably "democratic" society.

There is much yet that needs to be done in reconstructing the history of the education of laboring women. What can be said, however, is that while their formal schooling was limited, the breadth and depth of their efforts to overcome these limitations were in many ways heroic. Like Jane Addams, we may find that we have much to learn from their experiences.

The Professional Woman

Although some women practiced in a variety of professions prior to 1860 (407, 408), it was only after that date that women began to enter professional occupations in any great numbers. Several historical events contributed to that direction for women: the entry of women into teaching in the first half of the 19th century; the Civil War; the rise of women's colleges; and the pressure exerted by members of the woman's rights movement that began at the Seneca Falls Convention in 1848.

Like all social trends, women's interest in professional careers did not emerge overnight. The movement of women into teaching in the common schools, for example, had taken place over a 40-year period before the Civil War and was no longer uncommon. The middle years of the 19th century also saw women become increasingly part of the literary world as writers and poets. Similarly, professional women like Elizabeth Blackwell in medicine and Antoinette Brown in the ministry had pioneered in those fields by the 1850s. The Civil War, however, like its Revolutionary predecessor, provided ample opportunity for women to work in areas hitherto unknown to them. Harris notes, for example, that the "most important effect of the Civil War on women's work was to turn nursing into a profession for women" (308, p. 97). In the north, Elizabeth Blackwell, Dorothea Dix, Mary Ann Bickerdyke and Clara Barton pioneered in recruiting, training, and supervising the work of nurses; in the south, Sally Tomkins and Ella Newson did the same. Like teaching, nursing came to be associated with "women's work," and was viewed as yet another extension of women's nurturing role in the home.

Entry of women into what are sometimes called the "learned professions"—medicine, law, college teaching, the ministry, and somewhat later, science—took a good deal longer because these were fields almost entirely occupied by men and were perceived not as extensions of the private sphere but as a part of the public one. Not only were these professions outside the social norms for what was acceptable for women to do, they required advanced and specialized education in institutions that were closed to women.

The decades after the Civil War, however, saw an enormous increase in higher education for women. In part, women's opportunities for advanced education were a result of pressure from the 19th century women's rights movement which set out to demand equity for all women in a number of areas of life. Of perhaps more importance, however, was the financial distress of many institutions; lowered enrollments due to the Civil War and economic depressions caused college officials to begin to look to women to keep them in business (418). Thus, by 1870, Wisconsin, Michigan, Missouri, Iowa, Kansas, Indiana, Minnesota, and California all had coeducational state universities. Women in these schools, however, were predominantly enrolled in education or home economics courses and did not receive the same academic instruction as the men in those schools (308, p. 99).

The development of colleges for women, however, added a different dimension to women's education, and to their interest in professional careers. Elmira College (Elmira, New York), the first woman's college in the east, opened in 1854; by 1893, six of the "Seven Sister" schools—Vassar, Smith, Wellesley, Bryn Mawr, and Radcliffe—were granting degrees. What is significant about these schools for women, about which more will be said later, is that women who attended them did not regard the educations received there as preparation for homemaking (308, p. 99). Rather, students were interested in learning for its own sake, for preparation for teaching, and for work in a variety of professions. Nor were these schools designed for just any woman; as Harris notes, "The fathers of most of the girls had attended college and were businessmen or professionals. Scholarships went to daughters of professional families with modest incomes rather than to girls from working-class homes" (308, p. 99).

Attendance at a woman's college, however, did not guarantee entry into a profession or, indeed, entry into the job market at all. Despite the fact that more and more women between 1860 and 1920 entered the labor force (in 1900, 20.4% of all women were employed), the large majority of these were lower-class women who worked out of necessity. White, middle-class women had great difficulty finding a place in the professions of their fathers, for then, as earlier, social attitudes prevented them from gaining the knowledge that was considered to be most valuable.

Nevertheless, the woman's college did have a major role to play for those whose determination was undaunted by prevailing opinion. The women's colleges in the northeast, perhaps more than any other set of institutions, enabled women to develop their knowledge and skills free from competition with men in an atmosphere in which they were expected to make major achievements in a wide variety of areas of study. Many early examples of women in medicine, in law, in religion, in higher education and in science got their start in women's colleges and were able to pave the way for later generations. The women's college not only gave such women sound educations, it also provided employment—especially in college teaching and in science—for those who could not find positions elsewhere.

The price paid by many of these women was, however, high. For one thing, many of the first, second, and third generations of college women did not marry. In part, this was probably because social norms required that a middle-class white woman *either* marry or have a career. The bad news is that they were forced to choose; the good news was that they indeed did have a choice. Harris asserts that "after their exhilarating years at college, many women were far too committed to the pursuit of knowledge or the practical application of their educations to retreat willingly to the narrow confines of Victorian domesticity" (308, p. 102). It may also be the case that contemporary ideas about the "purity" of women and the Victorian antipathy toward sexual activity made marriage less than appealing to women who could, after all, support themselves.

Still, it is true that women did not make major inroads into the more male-dominated professions in these years. While women continued to enter schoolteaching and nursing and created the professions of home economics, library science, and social work, they were only a tiny percentage of those involved in medicine, law, theology, and college teaching. If one is looking for inequity in the practice of professions, it can be found here. However, it would also be a disservice to women's struggles to enter professional work to exclude from serious consideration their development of professions associated with their caretaking role. Indeed, study of the nature and impact of professional education of women in these fields is an area that requires significantly more attention than it has received to date.

Another area, one that is not often included in discussions of the professions but that offered a number of opportunities for women to participate in the public sphere, is business. Educational preparation for business did not, in the 19th century, necessarily require an advanced degree; rather, it required knowledge that could be gained through apprenticeship and experience. Of the eleven women listed in *Notable American Women* who lived and worked during the years from 1860 to 1920, none attended college, three came from poor families, two were southern blacks, eight were married and had children, and three worked in partnership with their husbands (308, pp. 119-120).

If, by the beginning of the 20th century, women had gained only the slightest foothold in the professional world, by the end of the century there is no profession not open to women, at least in some degree. There are still, however, large discrepancies between men and women in some fields, particularly those which center on mathematics and the physical sciences. Indeed, a current topic of debate in higher education today concerns the idea that, if women are to succeed in these professions, there should be more attention paid to educating them in single-sex institutions. Proponents of that belief argue that only in women's colleges and universities can the continued negative attitudes toward women as engineers, physicists, and computer scientists be effectively mediated. Clearly, women's colleges were successful a century ago in offering women the most valued knowledge of the day; perhaps the same can occur today.

The Working Girl

The distinction between the "laboring woman" and the "working girl" may be, in part, an artificial one, since both groups of women generally work out of need rather than self-advancement or altruism. However, in the history of the education of women, there are some differences between the two. Some of these differences lie in the nature of the social stereotypes of the two groups. The "laboring woman" is often perceived as less able intellectually and certainly lower on the scale of social prestige than the "working girl" (else why would she be laboring rather than working herself "up" to "better" jobs?) The image of the "working girl" is also somewhat more lighthearted and carefree than the image of the "laboring woman," whose work is often physically harder and has less chance of contact with powerful figures in the business. The image of the "laboring woman" is "blue collar," and associated with domestic service and/or labor movements; the image of the "working girl" is "pink collar," and associated with office work and management. The image of the "working girl" is, in addition, one in which the "girl" is only working for a while, making money until marriage and family come along or until some national emergency is over. In this regard, the experiences of "working girls" during the first and second world wars is instructive; Rosie the Riveter may have known how to make the ammunition, but when the soldiers came home she gave up her job on the assembly line and moved to the suburbs . . . for a while. William Chafe notes that while the number of women workers declined right after the second world war, by 1950 it had recovered to wartime levels (447, p. 519).

Like all stereotypes, of course, there is only a bit of truth to these images. Today, women in industrial jobs often make more money than women in office positions, and the woman whose job requires her to spend eight hours a day in front of a CRT may very well consider that work "labor" in many ways. Moreover, in the economic situation that we find ourselves at the end of this century, and with about 70% of the female population holding jobs, the "working girl" is quite likely to turn into the "working woman" who stays in the labor force for three decades.

Despite the discontinuities in the images of "laboring women" and "working girls," however, there are still differences in the education of these groups. Historically, the working girl was a clerical worker, either in an office or a shop or store, and had had a public school education through high school and sometimes additional education in business schools. That stratification was obvious among women's occupations is clear. Writing in 1929, Grace Coyle outlined the prevailing view:

> Domestic service and the less desirable types of factory
> employment vie with each other for the bottom place.
> The poorer kinds of store work usually come next,
> followed by the skilled factory work and ascending
> through telephone and selling positions to the clerical
> occupations (448, p. 181).

This stratification was in part related to the nature and degree of formal schooling available to various classes of women. The girl we have chosen to call the "working girl" was likely to have found instruction in commercial or business subjects in high school, well before the turn of the century (590, p. 30). He writes: "These courses were considered to have intellectual as well as vocational purposes, although one underlying aim clearly was to prepare young men for careers in business" (590, p. 30).

The growth of commercial business courses paralleled the growth in demand for white collar workers in the society. What was not emphasized at the time was that education for commercial purposes was, for all practical purposes, "women's education," because enrollments in these courses were predominantly female (590, p. 34). Unlike their counterparts in home economics, commercial teachers seldom had to actively promote their courses; indeed, home economics teachers often complained that "homemaking courses do not hold the girls in school" (590, p. 32). The lure of earning money at a respectable job clearly was a powerful incentive for many young women.

Differences in the education of laboring women and working girls also—and perhaps, more importantly—were related to the amount and nature of education available to women on the job. Because of rapidly changing technology in the office and store—from typewriter to telephone to computer—female office workers have had to learn to master an astonishing number of machines. Most of this knowledge was acquired not in school but through continuing education in the workplace. The changing nature of office work also increased opportunities for women to engage in semi-administrative duties, which put them closer to the decision-making process and thus on a higher rung of the corporate and social ladder.

Despite the educational opportunities that often separated the laboring woman from the working girl, female office employees seldom rose into the ranks of managers. Indeed, it was and is not uncommon for women with a wealth of experience in a particular company to do the same work as a manager, make countless decisions that affect the company and its employees, and carry a significant burden of other corporate responsibilities, yet continue earning the salary and maintaining the status of a secretary or administrative assistant. Education—that is, learning how to do the job—does not, in these instances, generally matter.

In considering the education of women for paid work, it is important to remember that although many women were taught a variety of skills for which they could be compensated in money, and although many women sought out for themselves the knowledge necessary to join with men in the workplace, vocational education for women differed in many respects from vocational education for men. For one thing, the jobs for which men and women were prepared were very often different. In speaking about industrial education for women, for example, Rury notes that "the work that women performed in industry was virtually the same as the work they did at home. The principal differences lay in the conditions under which work was performed" (590, p. 35). Secondly, women's work historically has been less valued than men's, women's salaries and wages have been (and continue to be) less than men's, and educational preparation for women's work has often been less rigorous or shorter. Thirdly, although women have occupied thousands of different kinds of jobs, they have with few exceptions until quite recently remained as workers rather than risen to supervisory or management levels. Even in the so-called "women's professions," managers and decision-makers have in large proportion been men.

At the same time, it is clear that women have taken every available opportunity to seek out, create, and obtain an education that would enable them to pursue work they wanted or needed to do, and in large measure, have seen that "independence [has been] placed within their grasp."

BIBLIOGRAPHY

General Works

299.   Abbott, Edith. *Women in Industry: A Study in American Economic History.* New York and London: D. Appleton, 1910.

300.   Ames, Azel. *Sex in Industry: a Plea for the Working Girl.* Boston: J. R. Osgood and Co., 1875.

301.   Baxandall, R., Gordon, L., and Reverby, S., eds. *America's Working Women: A Documentary History—1600 to the Present.* New York: Vintage Books, 1976.

302.   Brownlee, Elliot and Brownlee, Mary, eds. *Women in the American Economy: A Documentary History, 1675-1929.* New Haven: Yale University Press, 1976.

303.   Campbell, Helen. *Prisoners of Poverty, Women Wage-Workers, Their Trades and Their Lives.* Boston: Roberts Brothers, 1887.

304.   ———. *Women Wage-Earners: Their Past, Their Present and Their Future.* Boston: Roberts Brothers, 1893.

305.   Clark, Alice. *The Working Life of Women in the Seventeenth Century.* London: G. Routledge and Sons, 1919.

306.   Foner, Phillip. *Women and the American Labor Movement: From Colonial Times to the Eve of World War I.* New York: The Free Press, 1979.

307. Gutman, Herbert G. "Work, Culture, and Society in Industrializing America, 1815-1919." *American Historical Review 78* (1973): 531-588.

308. Harris, Barbara J. *Beyond Her Sphere: Women and the Professions in American History*. Westport, CT: Greenwood Press, 1978.

309. Henry, Alice. *Women and the Labor Movement*. New York: George H. Doran Co., 1923.

310. Hill, Joseph A. *Women in Gainful Occupations, 1870-1920*. Washington, DC: U.S. Government Printing Office, 1929.

311. Jones, Jacqueline. *Labor of Love, Labor of Sorrow: Black Women, Work, and the Family from Slavery to the Present*. New York: Basic Books, 1985.

312. Josephson, Hannah. *The Golden Threads: New England Mill-Girls and Magnates*. New York: Russell and Russell, 1967.

313. Kessler-Harris, Alice. *Women Have Always Worked: An Historical Overview*. Old Waterbury, CT: The Feminist Press, 1981.

314. ———. *Out to Work: A History of Wage-Earning Women in the United States*. New York: Oxford University Press, 1982.

315. MacLean, Annie M. *Wage-Earning Women*. New York: Macmillan, 1910.

316. ———. *Women Workers and Society*. Chicago: A. C. McClurg and Co., 1916.

317. Matthael, Julia A. *An Economic History of Women in America: Women's Work, the Sexual Division of Labor, and the Development of Capitalism*, Chs. 1 and 2. New York: Schocken Books, 1982.

318. Meyer, Annie Nathan, ed. *Woman's Work in America*. New York: Henry Holt and Co., 1891.

319. Reid, Robert L. *The Professionalization of Public School Teachers: The Chicago Experience, 1895-1920* (Ph.D. diss., Northwestern University), 1968.

320. Riis, Jacob. *How The Other Half Lives: Studies Among the Tenements of New York*. New York: C. Scribner's Sons, 1890.

321. Ruddick, Sara and Daniels, Pamela, eds. *Working It Out.* New York: Pantheon, 1977.

322. Sacks, Karen Brodkin and Remy, Dorothy, eds. *My Troubles Are Going to Have Trouble with Me: Everyday Trials and Triumphs of Women Workers.* New Brunswick, NJ: Rutgers University Press, 1984.

323. Smuts, Robert W. *Women and Work in America.* New York: Schocken Books, 1971.

324. Strober, Myra H. and Lanford, Audri Gordon. "The Feminization of Public School Teaching: Cross-sectional Analysis, 1850-1880." *Signs: Journal of Women in Culture and Society 11* (1986): 212-235.

325. Sugg, Redding. *Motherteacher: The Feminization of American Education.* Charlottesville, VA: University Press of Virginia, 1978.

326. Tentler, Leslie. *Wage-Earning Women: Industrial Work and Family Life in the United States, 1900-1930.* New York: Oxford University Press, 1979.

327. Theodore, Athena, ed. *The Professional Woman.* Cambridge, MA: Schenkman, 1971.

328. U.S. Women's Bureau. *Chronological Development of Labor Legislation for Women in the United States.* Bulletin No. 66-II. Washington, DC: U.S. Government Printing Office, 1929.

329. ———. *Negro Women in Industry.* Bulletin No. 20. Washington, DC: U.S. Government Printing Office, 1922.

330. ———. *The New Position of Women in American Industry.* Bulletin No. 12. Washington, DC: U.S. Government Printing Office, 1920.

331. ———. *The Immigrant Woman and Her Job, by Caroline Manning.* Bulletin No. 74. Washington, DC: U.S. Government Printing Office, 1930.

332. Walshok, Mary Lindenstein. *Blue Collar Women: Pioneers on a Male Frontier.* New York: Doubleday, 1981.

333. Weiss, Jane A., Ramirez, Francisco O., with Terry Tracy. "Female Participation in the Occupational System: A Comparative Institutional Analysis." *Social Problems 23* (1976): 593-608.

334. Wertheimer, Barbara Mayer. *We Were There: The Story of Working Women in America.* New York: Pantheon Books, 1977.

The Teaching Daughter

335. Beecher, Catharine. *An Essay on the Education of Female Teachers.* New York: Van Nostrand and Dwight, 1835.

336. Bernard, Richard M. and Maris A. Vinovskis. "The Female School Teacher in Ante-Bellum Massachusetts." *Journal of Social History 10* (1977): 332-345.

337. Buetow, H. "Historical Overview of Catholic Teacher Training in the U.S." *School and Society 100* (1972): 165-172.

338. Child, Lydia Maria. *The Freedman's Book.* Boston: Ticknor and Fields, 1865.

339. Clifford, Geraldine Joncich. "'Daughters into Teachers': Educational and Demographic Influences on the Transformation of Teaching into Women's Work in America." *History of Education Review 12* (1983): 15-28.

340. Collier-Thomas, Bettye. "The Impact of Black Women in Education: An Historical Overview." *Journal of Negro Education 51* (1982): 173-80.

341.   Crom, Robert D. "Recent Histories of U.S. Catholic
        Education." *History of Education Quarterly 14* (1974):
        125-126.

342.   Cuban, Larry. *How Teachers Taught: Constancy and Change
        in American Classrooms, 1890-1980.* New York:
        Longman, 1985.

343.   Donovan, Frances. *The Schoolma'am.* New York: Arno Press,
        1969. (Orig. pub., 1938.)

344.   Finkelstein, Barbara. "Governing the Young: Teacher
        Behavior in American Primary Schools, 1820-1880; A
        Documentary History" (Ed.D. dissertation, Teachers
        College, Columbia University), 1970.

345.   Fowler, Henry. "Educational Services of Mrs. Emma Willard."
        Journal of American History 65 (1978): 679-703.

346.   Fuller, Anna. "The Schoolmarm." In *Pratt Portraits.* New
        York: G. P. Putnam and Sons, 1892.

347.   Hoffman, Nancy. *Women's True Profession: Voices from the
        History of Teaching.* Old Westbury, NY: The Feminist
        Press and McGraw-Hill, 1981.

348.   Ihle, Elizabeth L. *Black Girls and Women in Elementary
        Education: History of Black Women's Education in the
        South, 1865-Present.* Harrisonburg, VA: James Madison
        University, WEEA Program, US DOE, 1986.

349.   Jensen, Joan M. "Not Only Ours But Others: The Quaker
        Teaching Daughters of the Mid-Atlantic, 1790-1850."
        History of Education Quarterly 24 (1984): 3-19.

350.   Jones, Jacqueline. "'The Great Opportunity': Northern
        Teachers and the Georgia Freedmen 1865-1873" (Ph.D.
        diss., University of Wisconsin), 1975.

351.   ———. "Women Who Were More Than Men: Sex and Status in
        Freedman's Teaching." *History of Education Quarterly 19*
        (1979): 47-59.

352.   ——. *Soldiers of Light and Love: Northern Teachers and
         Georgia Blacks, 1865-1873*. Chapel Hill: University of
         North Carolina Press, 1980.

353.   Jones, L. *The Jeanes Teacher in the United States: 1908-1933*.
         Chapel Hill, NC: University of North Carolina Press,
         1937.

354.   Kaufman, Polly Welts. "A Wider Field of Usefulness: Pioneer
         Women Teachers in the West, 1848-1854." *Journal of the
         West 21* (1982): 16-25.

355.   ——. *Women Teachers on the Frontier*. New Haven: Yale
         University Press, 1984.

356.   Mayo, Reverend A. D. "The Kitchen and the School-room."
         The National Teacher (1872).

357.   Melder, Keith. "Training Women Teachers: Private
         Experiments, 1820-1840." ERIC Document, ED 180 936,
         undated.

358.   ——. "Women's High Calling: The Teaching Profession in
         America, 1830-1860." *American Studies 13* (1972): 19-32.

359.   Morris, Robert C. *Reading, 'Riting, and Reconstruction: The
         Education of Freedmen in the South*. Chicago: University
         of Chicago Press, 1981.

360.   Nelson, Margaret K. "From the One-Room Schoolhouse to the
         Graded School: Teaching in Vermont, 1910-1950."
         Frontiers 7 (1983): 14-20.

361.   ——. "The Threat of Sexual Harassment: Rural Vermont
         School Teachers, 1915-1950." *Educational Foundations 2*
         (1988): 61-78.

362.   Oates, Mary J. "The Professional Preparation of Parochial
         School Teachers, 1870-1940." *Historical Journal of
         Massachusetts 12* (1984): 60-72.

363.   Perkins, Linda. "Quaker Beneficence and Black Control: The
         Institute for Colored Youth, 1852-1903." In Vincent P.

Franklin and James D. Anderson, eds., *New Perspectives on Black Educational History*. Boston: G. K. Hall, 1978.

364.   ———. "The Black Female American Missionary Association Teacher in the South, 1861-1870." In Jeffrey J. Cros and Flora J. Hatley, eds., *Black Americans in North Carolina and the South*, pp. 126-131. Chapel Hill: The University of North Carolina Press, 1984.

365.   Perko, F. Michael. "Schooling on the American Frontier." *History of Education Quarterly 26* (1986): 425-432.

366.   Quantz, Richard A. "The Complex Visions of Female Teachers and the Failure of Unionization in the 1930s: An Oral History." *History of Education Quarterly 25* (1985): 439-458.

367.   Rabinowitz, Howard N. "Half a Loaf: The Shift from White to Black Teachers in the Negro Schools of the Urban South: 1865-1890." *Journal of Southern History 40* (1974): 565-594.

368.   Rice, Elizabeth. "A Yankee Teacher in the South." *Century Magazine 40* (1901).

369.   Richardson, John and Hatcher, Brenda Wooden. "The Feminization of Public School Teaching, 1870-1920." *Work and Occupations 10* (1983): 81-99.

370.   Small, Sandra E. "The Yankee Schoolmarm in Freedman's Schools: An Analysis of Attitudes." *Journal of Southern History 14* (1979): 381-402.

371.   Vaughn-Roberson, Courtney Ann. "Sometimes Independent but Never Equal—Women Teachers, 1900-1950: The Oklahoma Example." *Pacific Historical Review 53* (1984): 39-58.

372.   Vinovskis, Maris A. "Trends in Massachusetts Education 1826-1860." *History of Education Quarterly 12* (1972): 501-530.

373. Willard, Emma. *A Plan for Improving Female Education* (reprint of 1819 edition). Middlebury, Vermont: Middlebury College, 1918.

374. Wofford, Kate V. *A History of the Status and Training of Elementary Rural Teachers of the United States, 1860-1930*. Pittsburgh: Press of T. Siviter and Co., 1935.

The Laboring Woman

375. Abbott, Edith. "Harriet Martineau and the Employment of Women in 1836." *Journal of Political Economy 14* (1906): 614-626.

376. Anderson, James D. *The Education of Blacks in the South, 1860-1935*. Chapel Hill: University of North Carolina Press, 1988.

377. Bank, Mirra. *Anonymous Was a Woman*. New York: St. Martin's Press, 1979.

378. Clifford, Geraldine Joncich. "'Marry, Stitch, Die, or Do Worse': Educating Women for Work." In Harvey Kantor and David Tyack, eds., *Work, Youth, and Schooling: Historical Perspectives of Vocationalism in American Education*, pp. 223-349. Stanford: Stanford University Press, 1982.

379. Davis, Allen F. "The Women's Trade Union League: Origins and Organization." *Labor History 5* (1964): 3-17.

380. Dodge, Grace, ed. *Thoughts of Busy Girls. Written by a Group of Girls Who Have Little Time for Study, and Yet Who Find Much Time for Thinking*. New York: Cassell Publishing Co., 1892.

381. Ewens, Mary. "The Leadership of Nuns in Immigrant Catholicism." In Rosemary Radford Ruether and Rosemary Skinner Keller, eds., *Women and Religion in America, Vol. I*, pp. 101-149. San Francisco: Harper and Row, 1981.

382.   Fetherling, Dale. *Mother Jones, The Miners' Angel: A
        Portrait.* Carbondale: Southern Illinois University Press,
        1974.

383.   Fox, Genevieve M. *The Industrial Awakening and the
        Y.W.C.A.* New York: Young Women's Christian
        Association, 1919.

384.   Henry, Alice. *The Trade Union Woman.* New York: D.
        Appleton and Co., 1918.

385.   Ihle, Elizabeth L. *Black Women's Vocational Education:
        History of Black Women's Education in the South,
        1865-Present.* Harrisonburg, VA: James Madison
        University, WEEA Program, US DOE, 1986.

386.   Larcom, Lucy. *A New England Girlhood, Outlined from
        Memory.* Boston: Houghton Mifflin, 1889.

387.   ———. "Lucy Larcom's Factory Experience." In Nancy F. Cott,
        ed., *Root of Bitterness*, pp. 126-129. New York: E. P.
        Dutton, 1972.

388.   Lerner, Gerda. "The Lady and the Mill Girl: Changes in the
        Status of Women in the Age of Jackson." In *The Majority
        Finds Its Past*, pp. 15-30. New York: Oxford University
        Press, 1979.

389.   Montgomery, David. "The Working Classes of the Pre-
        Industrial American City, 1780-1830." *Labor History 9*
        (1968): 3-22.

390.   Salmon, Lucy M. *Domestic Service.* New York: Macmillan,
        1897.

391.   Seller, Maxine. "The Education of the Immigrant Woman,
        1900-1935." *Journal of Urban History 4* (1978): 307-330.

392.   Smith, Timothy L. "Immigrant School Aspirations and
        American Education, 1880-1930." *American Quarterly*
        (1969): 523-543.

393.   Tyack, David and Lowe, Robert. "The Constitutional Moment:
        Reconstruction and Black Education in the South."
        American Journal of Education 94 (1986): 236-256.

394.   Valli, Linda. "Sisterhood and Solidarity: Workers' Education
        for Women, 1914-1984." *Educational Studies 17* (1986):
        44-49.

395.   Walkowitz, Daniel J. "Working-Class Women in the Gilded
        Age: Factory, Community and Family Life Among
        Cohoes, New York Cotton Workers." *Journal of Social
        History 5* (1972): 464-490.

396.   Webber, Thomas L. *Deep Like the Rivers: Education in the
        Slave Community, 1831-1865.* New York: W. W. Norton,
        1978.

397.   Wright, Carroll D. *The Working Girls of Boston.* Boston:
        Wright and Potter Printing Co., 1889.

The Professional Woman

398.   Bernard, Jessie. *Academic Women.* University Park:
        Pennsylvania State University Press, 1964.

399.   Blackwell, Elizabeth. *Opening the Medical Profession to
        Women.* New York: Schocken Books, 1977.

400.   Blake, John B. "Women and Medicine in Ante-Bellum
        America." *Bulletin of the History of Medicine 39* (1965):
        99-123.

401.   Bock, E. Wilbur. "Farmer's Daughter Effect: The Case of the
        Negro Female Professionals." *Phylon XXX* (1969): 17-26.

402.   Brumberg, Joan Jacobs and Tomes, Nancy. "Women in the
        Professions: A Research Agenda for American
        Historians." *Reviews in American History 10* (1982): 275-
        296.

403.   Carter, Susan B. "Academic Women Revisited: An Empirical
        Study of Changing Patterns in Women's Employment as
        College and University Faculty, 1890-1963." *Journal of
        Social History 14* (1981): 675-699.

404. Chadwick, James R., M.D. *The Study and Practice of Medicine by Women*. New York: 1879.

405. Chinn, Phyllis Zweig. *Women in Science and Mathematics: Bibliography*. Arcata, CA: Humboldt State University, 1980.

406. Clifford, Geraldine Joncich. "Women's Liberation and Women's Professions: Reconsidering the Past, Present, and Future." In John Mack Faragher and Florence Howe, eds., *Women and Higher Education in American History*, pp. 165-182. New York: W. W. Norton, 1988.

407. Dexter, Elisabeth. *Career Women of America, 1776-1840*. Francetown, NH: Marshall Jones Company, 1950.

408. ———. *Colonial Women of Affairs: Women in Business and the Professions in America Before 1776, 2nd ed. rev.* Clifton, NJ: Augustus Kelley Publishers, 1972.

409. Donnison, Jean. *Midwives and Medical Men: A History of Inter-Professional Rivalries and Women's Rights*. London: Heinemann, 1977.

410. Drinker, Sophie H. "Women Attorneys of Colonial Times." *Maryland Historical Magazine 56* (1961): 335-351.

411. Ehrenreich, Barbara and English, Deirdre. *Witches, Midwives and Nurses: A History of Women Healers*. Old Westbury, NY: Feminist Press, 1973.

412. Epstein, Cynthia Fuchs. *Woman's Place: Options and Limits in Professional Careers*. Berkeley and Los Angeles: University of California Press, 1971.

413. Finklestein, Barbara. "The Revolt Against Selfishness: Women and the Dilemmas of Professionalism in Early Childhood Education." In B. Spodek, O. N. Saracho, and D. L. Peters, eds., *Professionalism in Early Childhood Education*. New York: Teachers College Press, 1987.

414. Furnish, Dorothy Jean. "Women in Religious Education: Pioneers for Women in Professional Ministry." In Rosemary Radford Ruether and Rosemary Skinner

Keller, eds., *Women and Religion in America, Vol. 3*, pp.
311-338. New York: Harper and Row, 1986.

415. Garrison, Dee. "The Tender Technicians: The Feminization of
Public Librarianship, 1876-1905." In Mary S. Hartman
and Lois Banner, eds., *Clio's Consciousness Raised*, pp.
157-178. New York: Harper Torchbooks, 1974.

416. ———. *Apostles of Culture: The Public Librarian and American
Society, 1876-1920*. New York: The Free Press, 1979.

417. Ginzberg, Eli and Yohalem, Alice M., eds. *Corporate Lib:
Women's Challenge to Management*. Baltimore: Johns
Hopkins University Press, 1973.

418. Graham, Patricia Albjerg. "Women in Academe." In Athena
Theordore, ed., *The Professional Woman*, pp. 720-740.
Cambridge, MA: Schenkman, 1971.

419. ———. "Women in Higher Education: A Report to the Ford
Foundation." Ford Foundation Archival Report, 1977.

420. Haas, Violet and Perucci, Carolyn, eds. *Women in Scientific
and Engineering Professions*. Ann Arbor, MI: University
of Michigan Press, 1984.

421. Harris, Ann Sutherland. "The Second Sex in Academe." In
Elizabeth S. Maccia et al., eds., *Women and Education*,
pp. 161-192. Springfield, IL: Thomas, 1975.

422. Hedin, Barbara A. and Donovan, Joan. "A Feminist
Perspective on Nursing Education." *Nurse Educator 14*
(1989): 8-13.

423. Hennig, Margaret and Anne Jardim. *The Managerial Woman*.
Garden City, NY: Doubleday, 1977.

424. Hollis, Ernest V. and Taylor, Alice L. *Social Work Education
in the United States, The Report of a Study Made for the
National Council on Social Work Education*. New York:
Columbia University Press, 1951.

425. Hurd-Mead, Kate Campbell. *Medical Women of America: A
Short History of the Pioneer Medical Women of America*

and a Few of Their Colleagues in England. New York: Froben Press, 1933.

426. Kohlstedt, Sally Gregory. "In from the Periphery: American Women in Science, 1830-1880." *Signs: Journal of Women in Culture and Society 4* (1978): 81-96.

427. Lopate, Carol. *Women in Medicine.* Baltimore: Johns Hopkins University Press, 1968.

428. Lubove, Roy. *The Professional Altruist: The Emergence of Social Work as a Career, 1880-1930.* Cambridge: Harvard University Press, 1965.

429. Melosh, Barbara. *The Physician's Hand: Work, Culture and Conflict in American Nursing.* Philadelphia: Temple University Press, 1982.

430. Roberts, Mary K. *American Nursing: History and Interpretation.* New York: Macmillan, 1954.

431. Rosen, George. *A History of Public Health.* New York: M. D. Publications, 1958.

432. Rossiter, Margaret W. "Women Scientists in America Before 1920." *American Scientist 62* (1974): 312-323.

433. ———. "'Women's Work' in Science, 1880-1920." *Isis 71* (1980): 381-398.

434. Seymer, Lucy Ridgely. *A General History of Nursing.* London: Faber and Faber, 1954.

435. Shryock, Richard Harrison. "Women in Academic Medicine." In *Medicine in America: Historical Essays*, pp. 177-199. Baltimore: Johns Hopkins University Press, 1966.

436. Simeone, Angela. *Academic Women: Working Towards Equality.* New York: Bergin and Garvey, 1988.

437. Stern, Madeleine B. *We the Women: Career Firsts of Nineteenth-Century America.* New York: Schulte, 1963.

438. Stricker, Frank. "Cookbooks and Law Books: The Hidden History of Career Women in Twentieth-Century America." *Journal of Social History 10* (1976): 1-19.

439. Waite, Frederick C. *History of the New England Female Medical College, 1848-1874.* Boston: Boston University School of Medicine, 1950.

440. Walsh, Mary Roth. *'Doctors Wanted: No Women Need Apply': Sexual Barriers in the Medical Profession, 1835-1975.* New Haven: Yale University Press, 1977.

441. Williamson, Charles C. *Training for Library Services: A Report Prepared for the Carnegie Corporation of New York.* Boston: D. P. Updike, Merrymount Press, 1923.

442. "Women in Business; I." *Fortune* (July 1935).

443. "Women in Business; II." *Fortune* (August 1935).

The Working Girl

444. Acker, Joan and Van Houten, Donald. "Differential Recruitment and Control: The Sex Structuring of Organizations." *Administrative Science Quarterly 19* (1974): 152-163.

445. Barker, Jane and Downing, Hazel. "Word Processing and the Transfer of Patriarchal Relations of Control in the Office." *Capital and Class 10* (1980): 64-97.

446. Bird, C. "The Sex Map of the Work World." In M. H. Garskof, ed., *Roles Women Play*, pp. 39-61. Belmont, CA: Brooks/Cole, 1971.

447. Chafe, William H. "The Paradox of Progress." In Jean E. Friedman, William G. Slade, and Mary Jane Capozzoli, eds., *Our American Sisters: Women in American Life and Thought*, pp. 515-530. Lexington, MA: Heath, 1987.

448. Coyle, Grace L. "Women in the Clerical Occupations." In Viva B. Boothe, ed., *Women in the Modern World*, pp. 180-187. Philadelphia: The American Academy of

Political and Social Science, 1929. (Reprinted, 1974, by
Arno Press.)

449.   Davies, Margery. "Woman's Place is at the Typewriter: The
       Feminization of the Clerical Labor Force." *Radical
       America 8* (1974): 1-28.

450.   Feldberg, Roslyn L. "Comparable Worth: Toward Theory and
       Practice in the United States." *Signs: Journal of Women
       in Culture and Society 10* (1984): 311-328.

451.   Ferber, Marianne. "Women and Work: Issues of the 1980s."
       Signs: Journal of Women in Culture and Society 8 (1982):
       273-295.

452.   Fitzgerald, Louise F. and Shulman, Sandra L. "The Myths
       and Realities of Women in Organizations." *Training and
       Development Journal 38* (1984): 65-70.

453.   Fitzpatric, Blanche E. *Women's Inferior Education: An
       Economic Analysis.* New York: Praeger, 1976.

454.   Holland, Dorothy C. and Eisenhart, Margaret A. "Women's
       Ways of Going to School: Cultural Reproduction of
       Women's Identities as Workers." In Lois Weis, ed., *Class,
       Race, and Gender in American Education*, pp. 266-301.
       Albany, NY: State University of New York Press, 1988.

455.   Kanter, Rosabeth Moss. *Men and Women of the Corporation.*
       New York: Basic Books, 1977.

456.   ———. "The Impact of Hierarchical Structure on the Work
       Behavior of Women and Men." *Social Problems 23* (1976):
       415-430.

457.   Lee, Chris. "Training for Women: Where Do We Go From
       Here?" *Training 23* (1986): 26-40.

458.   Machung, Anne. "Word Processing: Forward for Business,
       Backward for Women." In Karen Brodkin Sacks and
       Dorothy Remy, eds., *My Troubles Are Going to Have
       Trouble With Me*, pp. 124-139. New Brunswick, NJ:
       Rutgers University Press, 1984.

459. Valli, Linda. "Gender Identity and the Technology of Office Education." In Lois Weis, ed., *Class, Race, and Gender in American Education*, pp. 87-105. Albany, NY: State University of New York Press, 1988.

460. Weis, Lois. "High School Girls in a De-Industrializing Economy." In Lois Weis, ed., *Class, Race, and Gender in American Education*, pp. 183-208. Albany, NY: State University of New York Press, 1988.

CHAPTER 5

Education for Civic Responsibilities and Action

We are the ones we have been waiting for.
—June Jordan

Although the roots of women's participation in the political, religious, and social activities of the community lay in their education for hearth and home, the actual experience of such participation was an education in itself. As has been noted elsewhere, the United States as a society has always had two important social ideas, the notion of rule by law rather than fiat, and the notion of voluntary association (142). If women have been excluded in large measure from legal status and consideration, they have excelled in terms of voluntary participation in civic life. Indeed, there are those who might argue that without such participation, life in the United States would have been quite different. In this chapter, we will look at some of the ways in which women were educated for participation in community life and learned how to exert influence on the public weal—an influence that is responsible for much of the periodic reform movements in U.S. history.

The Rebellious Woman

The conceptual dividing line between the rebellious woman and the woman reformer is sometimes blurred, in that frequently women have rebelled in order to reform. The distinction can be seen somewhat more clearly in the definition of differences between radical and cultural feminism (483, p. 531), or in Jill Conway's use of the terms "sage" and "expert" (486, pp. 402-403).

Ellen Willis defines the difference between radical and cultural feminism this way:

> Cultural feminism is essentially a moral, countercultural movement aimed at redeeming its participants, while radical feminism began as a political movement to end male supremacy in all areas of social and economic life, and rejected the whole idea of opposing male and female natures and values as a sexist idea, a basic part of what we were fighting (483, p. 531).

In the United States, rebellious women were much more likely to want to attack prevailing social norms outright, whether those norms were associated with education, with legal status, with access to the professions, or with labor rules. Rebellious women tended to place more emphasis on the similarity between males and females than on their differences. They argued that women are essentially *like* men, that the common humanity both shared entitled women to equal status and equal treatment. Rebellious women were at the forefront of early labor strikes; they demanded entry into colleges built for men; and they coalesced behind the first wave of the women's rights movement in 1848. Reforming women, on the other hand (about whom we will speak more later), were inclined to stress differences between men and women, usually claiming some form of inherent superiority for women, or, at least, insisting that "natural" characteristics of women made them peculiarly able to reform society and/or should become models for the direction taken by social reform efforts. Another way to flesh out this distinction has been taken by Jill Conway, who writes about two clearly distinct social types:

> The first is a borrowing from European culture, the type
> of the sage or prophetess who claimed access to hidden
> wisdom by virtue of feminine insights. The second is the
> type of the professional expert or the scientist, a social
> identity highly esteemed in American culture but
> sexually neutral (486, p. 402).

In these terms, the rebellious woman would more likely be the expert, utilizing extensive and precise knowledge to argue for change. As Conway notes, however, this type, this "rebellious" woman, has not captured the public mind and heart as has her more reform-minded sister.

Nevertheless, the rebellious woman has contributed significantly to women's experience and to the national well-being. The question that arises for us is, What part did education play in her rebellion?

One answer to that question is that increased access to a variety of forms of formal schooling gave some women the intellectual training and substance to begin to question the conditions under which they lived. Clearly, this was the case for Abigail Adams, who, though educated at home in her father's library, had read history and literature well beyond the norm of many of her contemporaries in the 18th century. While Adams never took her protests into the public sphere, she spoke and corresponded voluminously with her husband, John, and with friends like the colonial playwright, Mercy Warren.

Reading even portions of that correspondence provides one with a clear impression of a well-educated woman who not only questions the limitations imposed on her sex, but has a variety of suggestions to offer for improvement.

Similarly, but more publicly, Margaret Fuller in the 19th century exemplifies a rebellious woman whose writing (and public behavior) created a sensation while serving as a "major inspiration of the American feminist movement" (482, p. 75). The oldest child of a Harvard graduate and lawyer, Fuller was given a rigorous intellectual education by her father, and after his death earned her own living and helped to support her mother and younger brothers and sister by writing. Indeed, it is in her writing that the rebel is most clearly seen, for it is in her writing that she defended the arts in a still-Puritan society, attacked the causes of poverty in England and the United States, rallied to the needs of "pregnant slaves, overworked seamstresses and laundrywomen" (482, p. 83), and encouraged all women to be self-reliant citizens of independent thought.

If access to formal education, in schools or independently, was one path to rebellion, perhaps an even more direct one was the experience of oppression and degradation suffered by millions of slave women and women workers in a variety of fields, as well as by middle-class women stifling in the confines of domesticity. While there are too many to catalog in this volume, it can be said that for black and white women, wealthy and poor women, well-educated and ignorant women, experience was the teacher that led to rebellious acts. Clearly antagonistic toward the belief that women were weaker, less intellectually able, and generally more naturally dependent than men, rebellious women demanded equal rights with men in all areas of social, economic, and intellectual life.

The Reforming Woman

If the rebellious woman demanded immediate equality with men, sought her rationale in the humanity of all people, and wished to tear down from the outside the Puritan and patriarchal institutions that she saw as preventing equal treatment of women, the reforming woman was more apt to want to change existing conditions for women from the inside, using as her rationale the argument that women had both the experience and the nature to effect such changes in an orderly and humane manner. In addition, women reformers were interested in a variety of social ills affecting large numbers of people, both male and female, adult and child.

Harris notes that these women managed to argue their cases within the prevailing norms of "womanly" action and behavior. She writes that

> there was a real, if not irreconcilable, gap between
> women who advocated expanding the female role without
> challenging the domestic ideal and the founders of the
> woman's rights movement, who appealed to the
> egalitarian ideology of the Enlightenment and
> aggressively assumed roles normally restricted to males
> (308, p. 85).

While women have been active in reform movements of various kinds since the earliest days of the colonies, reform prior to the middle of the 19th century tended to be localized and carried out as an extension of women's family roles into the neighborhood. By the 1840s and 1850s, however, that role was being extended to the city, the state, and the nation as a whole. Like their more rebellious contemporaries, reforming women benefitted from access to formal schooling—certainly the common school and often female academies and early colleges that admitted women. Unlike the rebellious woman, however, the reformer was almost always a middle-class woman, usually but not always white, and able by virtue of her class status to afford the time to devote to a variety of causes. Indeed, in the 19th century it was the case that these women often were able to speak, travel, and write only because other, often lower-class, women took on some of their family responsibilities.

Another difference in the education of the reforming woman was that while experience was also often a "teacher," that experience might well have been vicarious rather than direct. The women who took on the abolitionist cause, for example, were primarily northern women who had not directly experienced slavery (the Grimké sisters, of course, were a major exception to that rule). Similarly, it was not necessary to have an alcoholic family member to be involved with the temperance movement, nor was it the case that those who worked to clean up the slums in the latter half of the century actually lived in them.

Still, the experience of being *involved* in reform movements was a powerful teacher, and lessons learned in travel, political strategy sessions, and public speaking were well utilized. In addition, the experience of working *with* other women, of sharing ideals and planning tactics, enabled reforming women to teach one another and to encourage the development of a more sophisticated understanding of public life. No one has yet studied the experiences of these women

to determine exactly what the nature of the "curriculum" was, or
what methods of "instruction" were most effective. One suspects,
however, that such a study could be conducted by analyzing the
voluminous correspondence carried on by women reformers for its
educational rather than its political content.

It is clear, however, that the reforming woman became a major
figure in 19th and 20th century life in the United States. In
discussing her distinction between the social type of the "feminine
sage" and the female "expert," Conway compares the experience of
Jane Addams, representing the "sage," and Julia Lathrop,
representing the "expert":

> What is interesting about the two types is that the sage
> had great resonance for American popular culture and
> was celebrated in endless biographies, memoirs and
> eulogistic sketches. Women who took on that role
> became great public figures, culture heroines known in
> households through the nation. But the woman as
> expert did not captivate the popular imagination and did
> not become a model of feminine excellence beyond a
> small circle of highly educated women of a single
> generation. Julia Lathrop, who was the pioneer
> strategist of the mental health movement, the innovator
> responsible for the juvenile court movement and the head
> of the first Federal Child Welfare Bureau which became
> the model for many New Deal welfare agencies, simply
> did not excite the faintest ripple of public attention
> during a lifetime exactly contemporaneous with Jane
> Addams (486, pp. 402-403).

It is also clear that both the rebellious woman and the
reforming woman did their work in the context of considerable
ridicule and public outcry. If the image of the reforming woman did,
indeed, find resonance in the public mind, so, too, was it easily
distorted into the image of the "do-gooder." Industrial magnates
were no more pleased at the prospect of having to pay higher wages,
employ fewer young children, or build safer factories than slave
owners were at the prospect of losing their source of free labor.
Similarly, husbands were not unanimous in applauding the work of
their wives outside the home, and educators were seriously in doubt
about the efficacy of offering higher education to women. In short,
the existing power structure did not bow to the reforming woman
with noticeable good grace.

In light of this fact, there grew up in the United States an alternative path to education and reform—the development of the woman's club movement. It is here that a number of determined and innovative actions were taken to provide not only self-help to women and community reform, but also to provide the solidarity of women's communities that has been a hallmark of women's education for three thousand years.

The Club Woman

If the common school was the institution that began the formal education of girls in the United States, the woman's club was the institution that, in the 19th and early 20th centuries, was primarily responsible for their education as adults (173, vol. 2, p. 453). Indeed, before women were routinely accepted into colleges and universities, the club movement provided a mechanism through which women could advance their own education and set about the reform of a variety of social ills.

The earliest women's associations in the United States date back to the 18th century, and were almost always philanthropic in motive, although the philanthropy in question was often educational. Such associations formed to open schools for poor girls, to provide relief for indigent women and children, to create work for unemployed women, and to provide food and clothing for those unable to obtain them on their own (173, vol. 2, pp. 454-455).

Other associations were formed as a result of the common school and female seminary movements. These most often were dedicated to the advancement of knowledge for women who, at the time, could not be admitted to college. Some associations were formed to encourage women to enter teaching, and to promote professional careers for women. Similarly, literary and missionary societies were formed to "elevate" women's cultural awareness and support the work of the church.

After the Civil War, the club movement achieved an extent and purpose that has lasted to this day. Although many women's clubs initially were established to encourage "cultural" attainment, they increasingly became directed toward social reform, and chief among the reforms in which these clubs engaged was the provision of education. In this period, however, the educational work emphasized a psychological shift in women's consciousness, a desire to encourage an independent spirit among women, and to increase their self-esteem. At the same time, women's clubs intended to improve social, economic, and political life in the community. The Civic Club of Philadelphia, for example, aimed to promote "by education and active cooperation, a higher public spirit and a better social order" (173, vol. 2, p. 459). Many of these organizations were large enough to include various "departments," including those devoted to government, education, and the arts.

In 1890, 63 delegates from 17 states met in New York City to form the General Federation of Women's Clubs, an organization which was granted a charter by act of Congress in 1901 (173, Vol. 2, p. 460). With this event, the work of women's clubs became a truly national movement. Among the work of women's clubs have been efforts to enact child labor laws, to promote compulsory education and reform schooling, to promote health and safety standards in industry and housing, to provide nonpartisan political information, to organize alumnae of colleges and universities, and to coalesce women of differing religious backgrounds. Women's clubs have not been the province of white, middle-class women only; indeed, the black women's club movement which paralleled its white counterpart, was one of the earliest and most effective mechanisms for promoting education for black children and for alleviating poverty among black citizens (see especially 506, 508, 512, 522, and 526).

Working with the twin goals of individual and social improvement, club women organized the awesome power of women's determination to better themselves and the society in which they lived. They did it, for the most part, within the context of women's traditional roles and outside of—although often related to—higher education. For this reason, in part, the educational impact of their work has not been the subject of mainstream educational history. Yet the contribution of women's clubs to the overall education of many women has been significant. Writing in 1912 about the effect of the early club movement, Jennie de la M. Lozier described several of its educational outcomes:

> It gives to woman, first, a sense of individuality; second, some conception of true democracy; third, sympathetic understanding; fourth, a development of the judicial faculty; fifth, a power of expression. In other words, the early club life may be said to have laid the foundation necessary for the proper development of that civic power with which organized womanhood should in the twentieth century prove its usefulness (527, Wood, pp. 50-51).

In short, women's clubs helped to change women's perceptions of themselves. It is interesting to note that from the 1860s to about World War II, the women's club movement existed side-by-side with other, much more well-known movements such as that for women's rights and, later, the Progressive Movement. While these latter movements have had significant social and political consequences, it is perhaps more interesting to a study of women's *education* in the United States that women's clubs have provided a nearly hidden source of educational activity and experience. It is the kind of activity that everyone knows about but no one pays much attention to. Thus, it is the kind of education perhaps most illustrative of women's education throughout much of history.

The Progressive Woman

The woman that can, with some accuracy, be called the "progressive" woman was, in large measure, a college-educated woman. Indeed, those who have been called progressive women in a historical context are usually *first-generation* college women who needed and wanted something useful to do with their hard-won higher educations.

The progressive woman came of age in the 1870s and 1880s, fresh from Vassar, or the University of Chicago, or any one of a number of small colleges in the midwest. She found a society undergoing massive social change—the effects of industrialization, of immigration, of developments in science and technology. She was also, however, still the product of a largely Victorian belief system regarding women's place. Thus, one of her problems was that although she had acquired an advanced education, one which, in many cases, *schooled* her to believe that she should both continue her education and apply it in useful ways, in most respects she was still expected to confine her efforts to home and family.

Jane Addams is perhaps the quintessential exemplar of this situation. Born into an upper-middle-class family in 1860, Addams graduated from Rockford Seminary in Illinois convinced that she had great things to accomplish; her problem was a lack of focus as to just what those might be. She had also acquired, both at home and at school, the widely held belief that women were morally superior to men and thus had a duty to use their energies to improve the conditions that men had created. Hymowitz and Weissman write that

> They were convinced that higher education would
> provide them an entry into the male world of politics and
> the professions. As women, they were already pure and
> pious; as college graduates they were also "rational,"
> "scientific," "intellectual" (148, p. 225).

Graduation often came as a "traumatic experience for these young women who had been educated to fill a place that did not yet exist. Their liberal education did not prepare them to do anything in particular, except perhaps teach, and the stylized, carefully edited view of life it gave them bore little relation to the actual world" (476, p. 79). Moreover, the views of her family concerning her life's work were in direct conflict with the views of her friends and fellow classmates. After a number of years of unspecified "illness" and travel as a companion to her stepmother, Addams went to Europe with her friend Ellen Starr and discovered the original London settlement house, Toynbee Hall. Returning to the United States, she and Starr bought an old house in Chicago and founded Hull House as the first settlement house in the United States.

It is not coincidental that Jane Addams was successful in establishing a settlement house; while her talents and skills were obviously enormous, she also began her work in a period of progressive reform that was worldwide. Thus, it can be said that the progressive woman was also a reforming woman *par excellence*. Nor is it coincidental that education plays a major role both in the background of their work and in their work itself. In a study of the lives of five progressive reformers, Ellen Lagemann asserts that education, taking place largely outside of formal institutions, is the key to predicting the achievement of the progressive woman in this period (538, p. 129). In many respects, the education of the progressive woman, according to Lagemann, is the kind of education that has been discussed throughout this chapter. Reviewing her work, Antler describes her vision of education as a continuous, cumulative, and life-long growth process; the "key to understanding how a person channels or shapes his/her potential and becomes an actor in the drama of his/her life" (530, p. 129). Thus, while formal schooling may play a part in this education, it is primarily a result of "informal relationships of everyday life, particularly through exchanges between family, friends, mentors and colleagues" (530, p. 129).

For the progressive woman, such education was instrumental in the achievement of identity and purpose. It was also the means by which they extended educational opportunities to others. Jane Addams, for example, developed her most innovative and effective educational programs at Hull House in ongoing interaction with poor women, immigrant women, and working women. Believing at first that she had much to offer them, she discovered instead that they had more to teach her (539).

At the beginning of this chapter it was asserted that the roots of education for civil responsibility and action lie in generations of education for hearth and home. Incorporated in that education is a strong sense of women's role as nurturer and caretaker, as well as the skills necessary to fulfill that role. In the United States, as elsewhere, however, that initial education for role has been extended and developed by schooling at many levels, as well as by apprenticeship, mentorship, interaction and support in women's communities, and by individual initiative. The social context in which women became the reformers of the nation is composed of wars, race and class injustice, economic manipulation of human beings, and the conversion of the United States from a collection of relatively homogeneous settlers to a pluralistic world power. In this context, the achievement of reform-minded but politically disenfranchised women has been astonishing. Considerably more work needs to be done on the peculiarly educational aspects of women's reform movements, but it is perhaps safe to say that education, in all its forms, has played a major role.

BIBLIOGRAPHY

The Rebellious Woman

461.   Cromwell, Otelia. *Lucretia Mott.* Cambridge, MA: Harvard University Press, 1958.

462.   Flexner, Eleanor. *Century of Struggle: The Woman's Rights Movement in the United States.* New York: Atheneum, 1971.

463.   Fuller, Margaret. "Women in the Nineteenth Century." In Miriam Schneir, ed., *Feminism: The Essential Historical Writings*, pp. 62-71. New York: Vintage Books, 1972.

464.   Griffen, Elizabeth. *In Her Own Right: The Life of Elizabeth Cady Stanton.* New York: Oxford University Press, 1984.

465.   Hays, Elinor R. *Morning Star: A Biography of Lucy Stone, 1818-1893.* New York: Harcourt, Brace and World, 1961.

466.   Hudspeth, Robert N., ed. *The Letters of Margaret Fuller.* Ithaca, NY: Cornell University Press, 1983.

467.   Kraditor, Aileen S. *The Ideas of the Women's Suffrage Movement, 1890-1920.* Garden City, NY: Doubleday, 1971.

468.   Lasch, Christopher. *The New Radicalism in America: 1889-1963.* New York: Alfred A. Knopf, 1965.

469.   Lerner, Gerda. *The Grimké Sisters from South Carolina: Rebels Against Slavery.* Boston: Houghton Mifflin, 1967.

470.   Lumpkin, Katharine Du Pre. *The Emancipation of Angelina Grimké.* Chapel Hill: University of North Carolina Press, 1974.

471.   McIntosh, Glenda Riley. *The Origins of the Feminist Movement in America: Forums in History.* St. Charles, MO: Forum Press, 1973.

472.   Melder, Keith. *Beginnings of Sisterhood: The American Woman's Rights Movement 1800-1850.* New York: Schocken, 1977.

473.   Murray, Judith Sargent. "Desultory Thoughts upon the Utility of Encouraging a Degree of Self-Complacency, Especially in Female Bosoms." *Gentlemen and Ladies Town and Country Magazine* (1784): 251-252.

474.   Oakley, Ann. "Feminism, Motherhood, and Medicine—Who Cares?" in Juliet Mitchell and Ann Oakley, eds., *What Is Feminism?*, pp. 127-150. New York: Pantheon, 1986.

475.   O'Neill, William L. "Feminism As a Radical Ideology." In Alfred F. Young, ed., *Dissent: Explorations in the History of American Radicalism*, pp. 275-300. DeKalb, IL: Northern Illinois University Press, 1968.

476.   ———. *Everyone Was Brave: The Rise and Fall of Feminism in America.* Chicago: Quadrangle Books, 1969.

477.   ———. *The Woman Movement: Feminism in the United States and England.* Chicago: Quadrangle Books, 1971.

478.   Ruether, Rosemary Radford. "Radical Victorians: The Quest for an Alternative Culture." In Rosemary Radford

Ruether and Rosemary Skinner Keller, eds., *Women and Religion in America, Vol. 3*, pp. 1-47. New York: Harper and Row, 1986.

479.   Schneir, Miriam, ed. *Feminism: The Essential Historical Writings*. New York: Vintage Books, 1972.

480.   Smith-Rosenberg, Carroll. "Beauty, the Beast, and the Militant Woman: A Case Study in Sex Roles and Social Stress in Jacksonian America." *American Quarterly 23* (1971): 562-584.

481.   Spender, Dale, ed. *Feminist Theorists: Three Centuries of Key Women Thinkers*. New York: Pantheon Books, 1983.

482.   Urbanski, Marie Mitchell Olsen. "Margaret Fuller: Feminist Writer and Revolutionary." In Dale Spender, ed., *Feminist Theorists: Three Centuries of Key Women Thinkers*, pp. 75-89. New York: Pantheon Books, 1983.

483.   Willis, Ellen. "Radical Feminism and Feminist Radicalism." In Jean E. Friedman, William G. Slade, and Mary Jane Capozzoli, eds., *Our American Sisters: Women in American Life and Thought*, pp. 531-555. Lexington, MA: Heath, 1987.

The Reforming Woman

484.   Bremner, Robert. *American Philanthropy*. Chicago: University of Chicago Press, 1960.

485.   Chambers, Clarke E. *Seedtime of Reform: American Social Service and Social Action, 1918-1933*. Ann Arbor, 1963.

486.   Conway, Jill K. "Women Reformers and American Culture, 1870-1930." In *Our American Sisters: Women in American Life and Thought, 2nd ed.*, pp. 301-312. Boston: Allyn and Bacon, 1976.

487.   Filler, Louis. *The Crusade Against Slavery, 1830-1860*. New York: Harper and Row, 1960.

488.   Gifford, Carolyn De Swarte. "Women in Social Reform Movements." In Rosemary Radford Ruether and

Rosemary Skinner Keller, eds., *Women and Religion in America, Vol. 1*, pp. 294-340. New York: Harper and Row, 1983.

489. Gilbertson, Catherine. *Harriet Beecher Stowe.* New York: D. Appleton Co., 1937.

490. Kenneally, James J. "Women and Trade Unions 1870-1920: The Quandary of the Reformer." *Labor History 14* (1973): 42-55.

491. Lerner, Gerda. "The Political Activities of Antislavery Women." In *The Majority Finds Its Past*, pp. 112-128. New York: Oxford University Press, 1979.

492. Levine, Daniel. *Varieties of Reform Thought.* Madison, WI: State Historical Society of Wisconsin, 1964.

493. Lutz, Alma. *Susan B. Anthony: Rebel Crusader, Humanitarian.* Boston: Beacon Press, 1959.

494. ———. *Crusade for Freedom: Women of the Antislavery Movement.* Boston: Beacon Press, 1968.

495. Melder, Keith. "Ladies Bountiful: Organized Women's Benevolence in Early Nineteenth-Century America." *New York History 48* (1967): 231-254.

496. Pease, Jane H. and Pease, William H. "The Role of Women in the Antislavery Movement." *Canadian Historical Association Historical Papers* (1967): 167-183.

497. Stearns, Bertha-Monica. "Reform Periodicals and Female Reformers, 1830-1860." *American Historical Review 37* (1932): 678-699.

498. Treudley, Mary B. "The Benevolent Fair: A Study of Charitable Organization Among Women in the First Third of the Nineteenth Century." *Social Service Review 14* (1940): 509-522.

The Club Woman

499.   Bailey, Nettie F. "The Significance of the Woman's Club
        Movement." *Harper's Bazaar 39* (March 1905): 204-209.

500.   Blair, Karen J. *The Clubwoman as Feminist: True
        Womanhood Defined, 1868-1914.* New York: Holmes and
        Meier, 1980.

501.   ———. *The History of American Women's Voluntary
        Associations, 1810-1960: A Guide to Sources.* Boston:
        Hall, 1988.

502.   Bryce, Mary E. "The Club as an Ally to Higher Education."
        Arena 6 (1892): 378-380.

503.   Cleveland, Grover. "Woman's Mission and Woman's Clubs."
        Ladies' Home Journal 22 (May 1906): 3-4.

504.   Davis, Elizabeth L. *Lifting as They Climb: The National
        Association of Colored Women.* (n.p. 1933).

505.   Diaz, A. M. "Women's Clubs: Their True Character." *National
        Magazine 3* (1896): 59-63.

506.   Dodson, Jualyne E. and Gilkes, Cheryl T. "Something Within:
        Social Change and Collective Endurance in the Sacred
        World of Black Christian Women." In Rosemary Radford
        Ruether and Rosemary Skinner Keller, eds., *Women and
        Religion in America, Vol. 3*, pp. 80-130. New York:
        Harper and Row, 1986.

507.   Granger, Mrs. A. O. "The Effect of Club Work in the South."
        *American Academy of Political and Social Science Annals
        28* (September 1906): 248-256.

508.   Hamilton, Tullia. "The National Association of Colored
        Women's Clubs" (Ph.D. diss., Emory University), 1978.

509.   Hawthorne, Hildegarde. "The General Federation of Women's
        Clubs: A Great Altruistic Movement." *The Century
        Magazine 80* (October 1910): 832-837.

510.   Henrotin, Ellen M. "The Attitudes of Women's Clubs and
        Associations toward Social Economics." *Bulletin of the
        Department of Labor 23* (July 1899): 501-545.

511.   Johnson, Helen Louise. "The Work of the Home Economics
        Department, General Federation of Women's Clubs."
        Journal of Home Economics 5 (April 1914): 153-155.

512.   Lerner, Gerda. "Community Work of Black Club Women." In
        The Majority Finds Its Past, pp. 83-93. New York: Oxford
        University Press, 1979.

513.   Lockwood, Florence. "Working Girl's Clubs." *Century
        Magazine 41* (March 1891): 793-794.

514.   MacLean, Annie M. "A Progressive Club of Working Women."
        Survey 15 (2 December 1905): 299-302.

515.   Matthews, S. "The Woman's Club and the Church."
        Independent 103 (3 July 1920): 12-13.

516.   Nobles, Katherine. "Club Life in the South." *Arena 6* (1892):
        374-378.

517.   Perkins, Linda M. "The Education of Black Women in the
        Nineteenth Century." In John Mack Faragher and
        Florence Howe, eds., *Women and Higher Education in
        American History*, pp. 64-86. New York: W. W. Norton,
        1988.

518.   Richmond, Mary E. "Working Women's Clubs." *Charities
        Review 6* (June 1897): 351-352.

519.   Severance, Mrs. Caroline M. "The Genesis of the Club Idea."
        Woman's Journal 33 (31 May 1902): 174.

520.   Sewall, May Wright. "Women's Clubs—A Symposium." *Arena
        6* (1892): 362-368.

521.   Talbot, Marion and Rosenberry, Lois I. *The History of the
        A.A.U.W., 1881-1931*. Boston: Houghton Mifflin, 1931.

522.   Terrell, Mary Church. "The History of the Club Movement."
       The Afro-American Women's Journal, 1940. Typescript
       copy in Mary Church Terrell Papers, Library of
       Congress.

523.   Ward, Mary Alden. "The Influence of Women's Clubs in New
       England and in the Mid-Eastern States." *American
       Academy of Political and Social Science Annals 28* (1906):
       205-226.

524.   Washington, Booker T. "The Club Movement among Colored
       Women of America." In *A New Negro for a New Century,
       Ch. 17.* Chicago: American Publishing House, 1900.

525.   Wells, Mildred White. *Unity in Diversity: The History of the
       General Federation of Women's Clubs.* Washington, DC:
       General Federation of Women's Clubs, 1953.

526.   Williams, Fannie Barrier. "Club Movement Among Negro
       Women." In John W. Gibson and William H. Crogman,
       eds., *Progress of a Race* (reprint of 1902 ed.). Miami:
       Mnemosyne, 1969.

527.   Wood, Mary I. *The History of the General Federation of
       Women's Clubs.* New York: Norwood, 1912.

528.   Wood, Mary I. "Civic Activities of Women's Clubs." *American
       Academy of Political and Social Science Annals 28* (1906):
       78-87.

The Progressive Woman

529.   Antler, Joyce. "Progressive Education and the Scientific Study
       of the Child: An Analysis of the Bureau of Education
       Experiment." *Teachers College Record 83* (1982): 559-591.

530.   ———. "Progressive Women." *History of Education Quarterly
       24* (1984): 129-135.

531.   ———. "The Educational Biography of Lucy Sprague Mitchell:
       A Case Study in the History of Women's Higher
       Education." In John Mack Faragher and Florence Howe,
       eds., *Women and Higher Education in American History*,
       pp. 43-63. New York: W. W. Norton, 1988.

532. Davis, Allen F. *Spearheads for Reform: The Social Settlements and the Progressive Movement, 1890-1914.* New York: Oxford University Press, 1967.

533. ——. *The Life and Legend of Jane Addams.* New York: Oxford University Press, 1973.

534. Duffus, Robert L. *Lillian Wald, Neighbor and Crusader.* New York: Macmillan, 1938.

535. Goldmark, Josephine. *Impatient Crusader: Florence Kelley's Life Story.* Urbana: University of Illinois Press, 1953.

536. Gordon, Linda. *Woman's Body, Woman's Right: A Social History of Birth Control in America.* New York: Grossman Publishers, 1976.

537. Kaufman, Polly Welts. *Boston Women and City School Politics: Nurturers and Protectors in Public Education, 1872-1905.* (Ph.D. diss., Boston University), 1978.

538. Lagemann, Ellen Condliffe. *A Generation of Women: Education in the Lives of Progressive Reformers.* Cambridge, MA: Harvard University Press, 1979.

539. Phillips, J. O. C. "The Education of Jane Addams." *History of Education Quarterly 14* (1974): 49-67.

540. Rousmaniere, J. "Cultural Hybrid in the Slums: The College Woman and the Settlement House, 1889-1894." *American Quarterly 22* (1970): 45-66.

541. Urban, Wayne. "Organized Teachers and Educational Reform During the Progressive Era: 1890-1920." *History of Education Quarterly 16* (1976): 35-52.

542. Wald, Lillian D. *The House on Henry Street.* New York: H. Holt and Co., 1915.

543. ——. *Windows on Henry Street.* Boston: Little, Brown, 1934.

CHAPTER 6

Defining the Educated Woman

If you complain of neglect of Education in sons,
What shall I say with regard to daughters, who every day
experience the want of it. . . . I most sincerely wish that
some more liberal plan might be laid and executed for the
Benefit of the rising Generation, and that our new
constitution may be distinguished for Learning and
Virtue. If we mean to have Heroes, Statesmen and
Philosophers, we should have learned women.
                                    —Abigail Adams, 1776

The definition of what it means to be an educated woman in
the United States has not changed very much in 350 years, and is
almost always associated with access to and acquisition of the
traditional liberal arts canon that for most of our history has been
given to boys of certain classes. Recently, that definition has come
into question; however, before discussing the current critique of what
it means to be an educated woman, it is necessary to know something
about formal higher education for women as it has developed in the
United States.

The Rise of Female Seminaries

Although a number of schools for girls appeared during the
colonial period—for example, one run by Ursuline sisters in New
Orleans was established in 1727, and one for Moravian girls in
Pennsylvania in 1742—probably the first genuine academy or
seminary for girls was the Young Ladies' Academy of Philadelphia
which opened about 1780. Characterized by a curriculum that
included reading and English grammar, penmanship, mathematics,
geography, some astronomy, and history, and by strict examinations
of proficiency in these subjects, the Academy was immediately
popular among prominent Philadelphia families. It was chartered in
1792, the same year that another famous girls' school, Sarah Pierce's
Litchfield Academy in Connecticut, was opened.
    Female academies (a term used often in the early years) or
seminaries (used more frequently in the 19th century) were at first
primarily schools designed to produce young women who would be
suitable companions for their husbands. In many respects, they were
"finishing" schools, teaching in addition to subjects such as those

listed above, a variety of "ornamental" skills such as music, painting, dancing, needlework, and French. Their students were the daughters of middle- and upper-middle-class families.

In 1821, however, Emma Willard opened the Troy Female Seminary in Troy, New York, which is generally considered to be the first institution of higher learning for girls that had a curriculum on a par with contemporary men's colleges. Emma Hart Willard, born in Connecticut in 1787, had begun teaching school at 17, and, along with Mary Lyon and Catharine Beecher, is credited with being a chief proponent of formal advanced schooling for girls. Her argument for higher education for women took advantage of the growing interest in the ideal of the republican mother. In her famous Plan for the Improvement of Female Education, submitted to the Governor of the State of New York, Willard put forth four major points:

1. It is the duty of government to provide for the present and future prosperity of the nation.

2. This prosperity depends upon the character of the citizens.

3. Character is formed by mothers.

4. Only thoroughly educated mothers are equipped to form characters of the quality necessary to insure the future of the republic (560, p. 6).

This was, of course, not a new argument in the 1820s. Willard, however, added several entirely new dimensions to it. First, she asked the state to support her school with public money. Second, she asserted that women were entirely capable of intellectual endeavors in any subject. And finally, she asserted that women should be educated for professional work, in this case, teaching.

Although the State of New York did not grant her funding request, together with her husband Emma Willard started the school anyway. Its curriculum included mathematics, science, modern languages, Latin, history, philosophy, geography, and literature. In addition, the Troy Seminary became one of the first schools to incorporate a systematic study of pedagogy and for most of the 19th century sent its graduates to all parts of the country to teach and to found schools of their own based on the Troy model. Among Willard's students were Catharine Beecher, who went on to become a leading national advocate of higher education for women, founded the Hartford Female Seminary in 1823 as well as a number of other seminaries in the east and midwest, and was responsible for removing a number of young women from the Lowell mills, training them as teachers, and sending them to establish common schools in the west.

Two other influential seminaries were the Ipswitch (Massachusetts) Female Seminary made famous by Zilpah Grant and Mary Lyon, and Mary Lyon's own Mt. Holyoke Female Seminary, which was one of the first schools to emphasize physical education for girls (546) and which later became Mt. Holyoke College. In addition, the Ipswitch pattern was duplicated in two other schools which are now colleges: Wheaton in Massachusetts and the women's course at Oberlin, which became the first coeducational institution to offer a college education to women.

Each of these schools was private and most catered to the daughters of middle-income families, although a number offered scholarships to those whose families could not afford to send them. All were founded on the premise that young ladies should be gently but rigorously taught to exemplify the 19th century notion of the moral woman who, as wife, mother, and teacher, was responsible for rearing generations of good citizens. In addition, however, these schools set forth a number of innovative ideas about teaching. Among these were a graduated curriculum, the cultivation of the emotions of children, discipline through love rather than by the rod, and the use of varied methods of instruction. Of particular interest in light of current debate on inquiry learning is the following advice from Zilpah Grant:

> Give scholars the opportunity to bring written questions
> to the teacher at every recitation, but not propose them
> orally in the class. Instead of answering these questions
> directly, let the teacher endeavor to excite, in reference
> to each of them, a spirit of inquiry in the class, and draw
> the answer from such of the class as can clearly express
> the idea, which she herself explains it so as to be adapted
> to the understanding of the least improved (357, p. 7).

The role of seminaries such as these for the promotion of education for women is an important one. More than the seminaries that taught "frivolous" subjects, these schools advanced the idea that women were not intellectually inferior to men, giving their students a thorough grounding in what was then a new idea about themselves—that they could, and should, make significant contributions to the life of the community and society. To a remarkable extent, schools such as the Troy Female Seminary influenced women who carried these ideas across the nation, and became exemplars to their children, grandchildren, and great-grandchildren (560). As a group, they defined one meaning of the educated woman for a century.

The Intellectual Woman

The seminary movement in the United States did more than produce good wives and teachers; it also helped to create a climate in which the life of the mind might be a viable option for women. Yet, negative attitudes toward the woman who devoted herself to intellectual pursuits were common in the 19th century, as they are still today. The ideal of the "true" woman, indeed, was antithetical to the notion of high intellect in women, and those who insisted on using their intellect were, in many respects, outside the pale.

The image of the woman as "thinker" has not been a popular one in any society, and it is perhaps even less so in a society dominated by egalitarian ideals. Observing this tendency, Abigail Adams wrote: "Oh, why was I born with so much sensibility, and why, possessing it, have I so often been called to struggle with it?" (568, p. 3). Similarly, Ocsar Wilde has written, "Contemplation is the gravest sin of which any citizen can be guilty" (568, p. 3).

There is a strong steak of anti-intellectualism in the United States, as is exemplified by our recurring bouts of populist and/or "know-nothing" politics. Nor have we, as a society, generated positive models of women as theorists. Although it has increasingly been "all right" to educate women for useful pursuits, still, we tend to distrust any person who concentrates on thinking as an occupation, and women most of all. Such women, as Conrad notes, are often considered "drab, aggressive, unnatural, unloved, and usually pitiful" (568, p. 5).

It is thus the case that not much study has emphasized the role of education in the life of the intellectual woman. Still, several scholars have attempted to analyze the lives and works of American intellectual women, particularly with respect to the development of feminist thought. In perhaps the most thoughtful of these, Susan Conrad carefully attempts to define the meaning of the term "intellectual" with reference to women:

> An intellectual's mark can be left on any "field" that
> calls for new hypotheses, speculations, interpretations,
> and generalizations. Data most conducive to intellectual
> activity has a quality that William James called "tough
> absurdity," a density and complexity that invites or
> defies one to notice discrepancies between ideas and

experience and, accordingly, to generate intellectual change. To become engaged in this process, and skilled in their chosen areas, intellectuals do not necessarily have to pass through institutions of higher learning or be affiliated with other institutions; they need be "professionals" only in the conscious mastery of their subject that characterizes professional work. This distinction is especially important with reference to women intellectuals [of the early 19th century], to whom many professions, supposedly congenial to intellectual activity, were closed (568, pp. 8-9).

The education of the intellectual woman thus often begins, not with schooling, but, as John Dewey observed, with a sense of discomfort or disjunction—in short, with a problem. Something is wrong. American intellectual women have not always been feminists, but the growing awareness of women's "place" that emerged in the 19th century in the context of abolition and in the 20th century in the context of the civil rights movement has served to create the conditions in which feminists have often been intellectuals. And in many instances, American intellectual women have focused on education—defined broadly—as a key factor in healing the social disjunction between women's place and women's lives.

Thus, for example, the women described by Alice Rossi in *The Feminist Papers* (570), all of whom in one way or another contributed to the intellectual development of feminism, all focus on the role of education in women's lives. Indeed, *The Feminist Papers* can be said to be, in part, a book of educational plans for women. Similarly, Dale Spender's *Feminist Theorists: Three Centuries of Key Women Thinkers*, in discussing the lives of major contributors to the feminist movement, also repeatedly refers to their ideas on education for women.

The role of the intellectual woman in defining what it means to be an educated woman has been one that consistently questioned the *status quo*, that encouraged or demanded increasing access to higher formal education for women, and that analyzed the ideal of the "true" woman in terms of its relation to reality. This work has focused not only on women's moral or spiritual qualities, but on their rational capacities and their ability to combine reason and feeling. If the intellectual woman has not had an honored place in American society, she clearly has had an important one; for it is often the person who asks the unexpected questions who creates the conditions in which change can occur.

The Rise of the High School

Although Tyack and Hansot describe the early history of the high school as "still obscure" (172, p. 115), Woody traces the evolution of secondary education for girls from the early part of the 19th century to his own writings in the early part of the 20th (173, Vol. 1, pp. 519-551). Developing at the same time as female seminaries, the major difference between early high schools for girls and female academies is that high schools were publicly supported and tended to emphasize academic rather than "ornamental" instruction.

Secondary education institutions specifically for girls emerged in the midst of a controversy over coeducation. In Worcester, Massachusetts, for example, there was some discussion about whether or not to open the Latin Grammar School to girls; that plan was defeated, however, and what is probably the first girl's high school was opened there in 1824. In Boston in 1826 a similar school was opened with 130 students. Like many early secondary schools for girls, it was considered "experimental." Woody writes: "The school was immensely popular; indeed, as Quincy said, it was 'an alarming success,' and was therefore abolished in 1828" (173, Vol. 1, p. 520). Clearly, the debate over the efficacy of offering higher education to girls was far from settled.

The public high school for girls was intended to provide an extension of common school education, to ensure that young women were suitably educated for their private roles in life, and to prepare teachers for the common schools. Many high schools in the first half of the 19th century offered courses in teaching, and some in child development. By the latter half of the century, high schools were also engaged in preparing young women for college, but initially they were terminal institutions for girls (173, Vol. 1, p. 531). Many of these schools were organized on the mutual instruction or monitorial plan, an extremely popular system that had, as one of its virtues, economy. Woody quotes a description of it as it was implemented in the Girls' High School in Boston:

> The government of this school is vested in a set of books, in which is recorded an accurate and minute account of every scholar's performances, deportment, absence, and tardiness; and at the end of each quarter, she is advanced to a higher, or degraded to a lower, section or seat, as this record shall appear in her favor or against her. The whole business is regulated by fixed principles, that are well understood; and every individual is, literally speaking, the artificer of her own rank, which is

> affected by every exercise she performs, and by every
> error she commits, either in recitation or conduct.
> Everything depends upon numerical calculation; and,
> were it expedient, the school might be classed by the
> scholars themselves (173, Vol. 1, p. 532).

It is perhaps not surprising that Tyack and Hansot allude to contemporary conservatives who "relish nostalgic images of a golden age, with dignified temples of learning in which the teachers were scholars, the pupils were studiously preparing for college, the academic mission of the institution was simple and strong, and the public well satisfied with its creation" (172, p. 115)!

The development of public high schools, for boys as well as girls, occurred mainly in urban areas that had sufficient taxing ability to support them. Indeed, coeducation was perhaps more an economic than a social justice solution to higher education for girls. In addition, the common schools were coeducational, and extending that practice did not appear to be terribly *avant garde*.

High schools were not unopposed by community leaders. In fact, many people, from all walks of life, had complaints about them. For some, public secondary education catered to the wealthy; for others, they were too diverse in their populations, or presented unfair competition to private schools. Debates about the nature of the curriculum, the gender and qualifications of teachers, the problem of trying to educate all races and classes, and funding raged for a number of decades. Indeed, in the face of all the controversy, it might seem surprising that they took root at all (172, pp. 118-119).

By the latter half of the 19th century, however, coeducational high schools were the norm. Attrition, however, was high, since secondary education was not compulsory and one could conceivably earn a decent living without it. Girls, however, continued in school longer than boys, and were, by the beginning of the 20th century, a majority of the high school population. This fact was the cause of considerable consternation among educational policy-makers, who determined finally that its cause was the feminization of schooling, in particular, the presence of so many female teachers. Known as "the woman peril," this argument was made most forcefully by Adm. F. E. Chadwick:

> Women teachers have "had so evil an effect upon the
> manhood of the country, on the qualities that go for the
> making of the masculine character, that it is more than
> full time to consider most seriously this great and vital
> question." In spite of "all the claims of the feminist

movement," men must "do the main work of the world:
build and handle steamships and railways, command
armies and fleets, fight our battles, tunnel our
mountains and make our steel." No woman can
adequately train the "force of character" necessary for
men because "the masculine and feminine natures are as
far apart as the poles." Therefore, to subject a boy to
women teachers "at his most impressionable, character-
forming age is to render violence to nature"; it can only
"result in a feminized manhood, emotional, illogical,
noncombatative" (172, p. 155).

Experiments with sex-segregated classes, and then sex-segregated
vocational tracks, were conducted in the early years of the 20th
century. They did not, however, either achieve desired retention of
boys or flourish as pedagogical innovations; by the 1930s, public
coeducational secondary education was the norm in the United States,
and girls were reasonably prepared for both college and the
workforce.

In terms of extending public education for girls from a large
variety of backgrounds, the high schools were a success. They were
not, however, the answer to a definition of the educated woman.
Nor were they, as some contemporary critics have pointed out,
necessarily the best mechanism for educating women; indeed, recent
scholarship has documented the several ways in which the
educational experiences that girls have in school are quite different
from the educational experiences of boys (799). Still, the public high
school provided a base of formal schooling for girls that did not exist
prior to its emergence. That base was the platform on which young
women launched the effort to obtain a college education.

The College Woman

Probably more has been written about the struggle for,
experience of, and consequences of higher education for women than
about any other single aspect of women's education. Indeed, the
phrase "women's education" is frequently synonymous in the
literature with formal education at the college level, to the extent
that historians of women's education have, for the most part,
neglected other important aspects of the overall education of girls.

In part, this is the result of a general public assumption that
education equals schooling. It is also, however, in part the result of a
far broader Western assumption that the acquisition of knowledge
normally taught at the college level is what separates "educated"

people from all others. The definition of an "educated woman" thus differs little, in this respect, from the definition of an "educated person." Since higher education generally is, according to some, predicated on male models of interpreting the world, this definition of the educated person may be inadequate (799, 801). That argument, however, can be saved for the next chapter.

For our purposes here, the era of the "college woman" can be said to have begun in 1837, when Oberlin College first granted a baccalaureate degree to a woman. Oberlin has been rightly celebrated for its leading liberal philosophy regarding the higher education of women and blacks. It is well to remember, however, that when Lucy Stone graduated shortly thereafter, she was unable to read her graduation address because it was not permissible for women to speak in public.

There is too much written about the evolution of higher education for women to recount many details here. Several characteristics of that education can, however, be summarized. First, the same debates about the advisability of educating females "beyond their sphere" were present in the struggle of women to achieve access to higher education as were present with respect to elementary and secondary education. Indeed, those debates were perhaps more vociferous when it came to higher education, both in terms of negative attitudes about women's inherent intellectual abilities and in terms of the "damage" that might be done to the family if women were allowed the kind of education that was increasingly necessary for entry into the professions. Second, there was (and is, again) a spirited debate about whether or not single-sex institutions were better for women (618). Clearly, women's colleges appear to have been an advantage for women aspiring to professional careers. However, it is possible that the family backgrounds of those women who attended private women's colleges also had a bearing on their eventual life patterns. Women's colleges, like private men's schools, were designed to educate an elite leadership. That they fulfilled their promise is clearly a credit to them but not necessarily a surprising outcome.

Third, where women were accepted into coeducational colleges and universities, they often suffered discrimination. Barbara Solomon, for example, writes that at the University of Wisconsin, women admitted to fill slots left empty by male participation in the Civil War often had to stand in the classroom until the remaining males were seated. Similarly, at the University of Chicago, when women began earning more Phi Beta Kappa awards than men, a separate (and lower) women's division was created for them (656).

Fourth, acceptance of women into coeducational colleges was not always done on an equal basis with men. Even where schools, such as Stanford, began accepting women in equal numbers, that practice was altered to a three-men-for-each-woman ratio (656).

Finally, women then as now have disproportionately majored in "female-oriented" subjects, notably literature and romance languages, as well as in those subjects related to the women's professions of teaching, nursing, and social work. Whether or not this should be a matter of concern is, itself, the subject of a great deal of debate. It is the case, however, that since women have gained access to a number of higher paying professions, the attraction of the most able women into the women's professions has become something of a problem.

Of particular interest, perhaps, in an analysis of the experience of the college woman, is the effect higher education had on women's lives. A good deal has been written about the ways in which college altered the life-cycle of women and the nature of families in the United States. One aspect of this study (described above) relates to the tension experienced by many female college graduates in terms of what Jane Addams called the "family claim." Another is the fact that a large number, although not a majority, of the first generations of female college women did not marry, or if they did, chose not to have children. This was, of course, viewed with considerable alarm by many who were opposed to college educations for women in the first place. In this regard, it is interesting to note that as far back as Plato's plan for the education of female guardians, there has been a belief that the family responsibilities of women will result in less time and energy for them to devote to other pursuits. For Plato, the recommendation was simple: abolish the family. For the generations since then, the struggle to balance family and work or education has continued to plague women, whether highly educated or not. Even in the 1990s, after three waves of the women's movement and the normative presence of the two-earner household, women still have that problem to deal with.

Clearly, access to higher education for women has steadily increased in the past century. Today, many young women—along with their brothers—believe that without a college education, there is little life of value to contemplate. Indeed, one is constrained to wonder whether the society's interest in credentialling that vests all of its educational "eggs" in the college basket has not eradicated the possibility of other, equally valuable, means of becoming "educated." Women today who wish to engage in the "good life" have very little choice about the nature of their education; the process of a relatively slow and thoughtful self-education that characterized some of the best female minds of the 19th century seems anathema today. Yet, it is just possible that such an education might have a salutary effect on women's contributions to themselves, their families, and the society as a whole.

All that notwithstanding, the entry of women into college on a large scale continues to play a major role in defining the educated woman. In the past 25 years, however, the development of Women's Studies as an area of scholarship has had a significant impact on the *redefinition* of what it means to be an educated woman, indeed, an educated person. It is to these ideas that we turn in Chapter 7.

BIBLIOGRAPHY

The Rise of Female Seminaries

544. Allmendinger, David F., Jr. "Mount Holyoke Students Encounter the Need for Life-Planning, 1837-1850." *History of Education Quarterly 19* (1979): 27-46.

545. Brickley, Lynne Templeton. *Sarah Pierce's Litchfield Female Academy, 1792-1833, Litchfield, Connecticut.* (Ed.D. diss., Harvard University), 1985.

546. Davenport, Joanna. "The Eastern Legacy: The Early History of Physical Education for Women." *Quest 32* (1980): 226-236.

547. Gilchrist, Beth B. *The Life of Mary Lyon.* Boston: Houghton Mifflin, 1910.

548. Gordon, Ann G. "The Young Ladies Academy of Philadelphia." In Carol Ruth Berkin and Mary Beth Norton, eds., *Women of America: A History*, pp. 68-91. Boston: Houghton Mifflin, 1979.

549. Lansing, Marion, ed. *Mary Lyon as Seen Through Her Letters.* Boston: 1937.

550. Lloyd, S. M. *A Singular School: Abbott Academy.* Hanover, NH: University Press of New England, 1979.

551. Lord, John. *The Life of Emma Willard.* New York: D. Appleton and Company, 1873.

552. Lutz, Alma. *Emma Willard: Daughter of Democracy.* Boston: 1929.

553. McClelland, Clarence P. "The Education of Females in Early Illinois." *Journal of the Illinois State Historical Society 36* (1943): 378-407.

554. Melder, Keith. "Mask of Oppression: The Female Seminary Movement in the United States." *New York History 55* (1974): 260-279.

555. Peabody, Elizabeth. *Record of a School, Exemplifying the General Principles of Spiritual Culture.* Boston: James Munroe and Co., 1835.

556. Roberts, Josephine. "Elizabeth Peabody and the Temple School." *New England Quarterly 15* (1942): 497-508.

557. Rota, Tiziana. *Between 'True Women' and 'New Women': Mount Holyoke Students, 1837-1908.* (Ph.D. diss., University of Massachusetts), 1983.

558. Savin, Marion B. and Harold J. Abrahams. "The Young Ladies' Academy of Philadelphia." *History of Education Journal 8* (1956): 58-67.

559. Scott, Anne Firor. "What, Then, is the American: This New Woman?" *Journal of American History 65* (1978): 679-703.

560. ———. "The Ever Widening Circle: The Diffusion of Feminist Values from the Troy Female Seminary, 1822-1872." *History of Education Quarterly 19* (1979): 3-25.

561. Shephard, William. "Buckingham Female Collegiate Institute." *William and Mary Quarterly 20* (1940): 167-193.

562. Sklar, Kathryn Kish. "The Founding of Mount Holyoke College." In Carol Ruth Berkin and Mary Beth Norton, eds., *Women of America: A History*, pp. 177-210. Boston: Houghton Mifflin, 1979.

563.   Stevenson, Louise L. "Sarah Porter Educates Useful Ladies,
        1847-1900." *Winterthur Portfolio 18* (1983): 39-59.

564.   Tharp, Louise Hall. *Until Victory: Horace Mann and Mary
        Peabody.* Boston: Little, Brown, 1953.

565.   Vanderpoel, Emily Noyes. *Chronicles of a Pioneer School from
        1792 to 1833: Being the History of Miss Sarah Pierce and
        Her Litchfield School.* Cambridge, MA: University Press,
        1903.

566.   ———. *More Chronicles of a Pioneer School, from 1792 to 1833,
        Being Added History on the Litchfield Female Academy
        Kept by Miss Sarah Pierce and her Nephew, John Pierce
        Brace.* New York: Cadmus Book Shop, 1927.

567.   Willard, Emma. *The Advancement of Female Education.* Troy,
        NY: 1833.

The Intellectual Woman

568.   Conrad, Susan. *Perish the Thought: Intellectual Women in
        Romantic America, 1830-1860.* New York: Oxford
        University Press, 1976.

569.   Rosenberg, Rosalind. *Beyond Separate Spheres: Intellectual Roots
        of Modern Feminism.* New Haven: Yale University Press,
        1982.

570.   Rossi, Alice S., ed. *The Feminist Papers: From Adams to de
        Beauvoir.* New York: Bantam Books, 1974.

571.   Schramm, Sarah Slavin. *Plow Women Rather Than Reapers: An
        Intellectual History of Feminism in the United States.*
        Metuchen, NJ: The Scarecrow Press, 1979.

572.   Spender, Dale. *Women of Ideas and What Men Have Done to
        Them.* London: Routledge and Kegan Paul, 1982.

573.   Vicinus, Martha. *Independent Women: Work and Community for
        Single Women, 1850-1920.* Chicago: University of Chicago
        Press, 1985.

574.   ———. "Liberty, a Better Husband. Single Women in America: The Generations of 1780-1840." *Signs: Journal of Women in Culture and Society 11* (1986): 411-414.

The Rise of the High School

575.   Anderson, James D. "The Historical Development of Black Vocational Education." In Harvey Kantor and David B. Tyack, eds., *Work, Youth, and Schooling: Historical Perspectives on Vocationalism in American Education*, pp. 180-222. Stanford: Stanford University Press, 1982.

576.   Armstrong, J. E. "The Advantages of Limited Sex Segregation in the High School." *School Review 18* (1910): 339-49.

577.   Barnett, Evelyn Brooks. "Nannie Burroughs and the Education of Black Women." In Sharon Harley and Bosalyn Terborg-Penn, eds., *The Afro-American Woman: Struggles and Images*, pp. 97-108. Fort Washington, NY: Kennikat Press, 1978.

578.   Burstall, Sara A. *The Education of Girls in the United States.* New York: Arno Press and The New York Times, 1971. (Orig. pub: London: Swan Sonnenschein and Co./New York: Macmillan, 1894).

579.   ———. *Impressions of American Education in 1908.* London: Longmans, Green, 1909.

580.   Caliver, Ambrose. *Secondary Education for Negroes.* Bureau of Education, Bulletin no. 17, 1932.

581.   Chadwick, F. E. "The Woman Peril in American Education." *Educational Review 47* (1914): 115-117.

582.   Clifford, Geraldine Jonich. "Home and School in 19th Century America: Some Personal-History Reports from the United States." *History of Education Quarterly 18* (1978): 3-34.

583.   DuFour, Richard P. "The Exclusion of Female Students from the Public Secondary Schools of Boston, 1820-1920" (Ed.D. diss., Northern Illinois University, 1981).

84. Kaestle, Carl F. *The Evolution of an Urban High School System: New York City, 1750-1850.* Cambridge, MA: Harvard University Press, 1973.

585. Kantor, Harvey and Tyack, David, eds. *Work, Youth, and Schooling: Historical Perspectives of Vocationalism in American Education.* Stanford: Stanford University Press, 1982.

586. Keller, Arnold Jack."An Historical Analysis of the Arguments for and against Coeducational Schools in the United States" (Ed.D. diss., Teachers College, Columbia University), 1971.

587. Lazerson, Marvin. *Origins of the Urban School: Public Education in Massachusetts, 1870-1915.* Cambridge, MA: Harvard University Press, 1971.

588. Maxwell, John Clinton. "Should the Education of Boys and Girls Differ: A Half-Century of Debate, 1870-1920" (Ph.D. diss., University of Wisconsin, 1966).

589. Powers, Jane Bernard. "The 'Girl Question' in Education: Vocational Training for Young Women in the Progressive Era" (Ph.D. diss., Stanford University, 1986).

590. Rury, John L. "Vocationalism for Home and Work: Women's Education in the United States, 1880-1930." *History of Education Quarterly 24* (1984): 21-44.

The College Woman

591. Antler, Joyce. "'After College, What?': New Graduates and the Family Claim." *American Quarterly 32* (1980): 409-434.

592. ———. "Feminism as Life-Process: The Life and Career of Lucy Sprague Mitchell." *Feminist Studies 7* (1981): 134-157.

593. Astin, Helen S. and Hirsch, Werner Z., eds. *The Higher Education of Women: Essays in Honor of Rosemary Park.* New York: Praeger, 1978.

594.   Berry, Mary Frances. "Blacks in Predominantly White
        Institutions of Higher Learning." In *The State of Black
        America*. Washington, DC: National Urban League,
        1983.

595.   Bixler, Julius. "Shall We Let the Ladies Join Us?" *American
        Scholar 4* (1935): 474-483.

596.   Blandin, I. M. E. *Higher Education of Women in the South
        Prior to 1860*. New York: 1909.

597.   Boas, Louise S. *Women's Education Begins: The Rise of
        Women's Colleges*. Norton, MA: Wheaton College Press,
        1935.

598.   Bowles, Frank and DeCosta, Frank A. *Between Two Worlds:
        A Profile of Negro Higher Education*. New York:
        McGraw-Hill, 1971.

599.   Cole, Arthur C. *A Hundred Years of Mount Holyoke College:
        The Evolution of an Educational Ideal*. New Haven: Yale
        University Press, 1940.

600.   Conable, Charlotte Williams. *Women at Cornell: the Myth of
        Equal Education*. Ithaca, NY: Cornell University Press,
        1977.

601.   Conway, Jill K. "The First Generation of American College
        Women" (Ph.D. diss., Harvard University), 1968.

602.   ———. "Perspectives on the History of Women's Education in
        the United States." *History of Education Quarterly 14*
        (1974): 1-12.

603.   Cookingham, Mary E. "Combining Marriage, Motherhood and
        Jobs Before World War II: Women College Graduates,
        Classes of 1905-1935." *Journal of Family History 9*
        (1984): 178-195.

604.   Cooper, Anna Julia. "The Higher Education of Women." In
        *Black Women in Nineteenth-Century American Life: Their
        Words, Their Thoughts, Their Feelings*. University Park:
        Pennsylvania State University Press, 1976.

605. Cross, Barbara. *The Educated Woman in America: Selected Writings of Catharine Beecher, Margaret Fuller, and M. Carey Thomas.* New York: Teachers College Press, 1965.

606. Curti, Merle. "The Education of Women." In *Social Ideas of American Educators.* Paterson, NJ: Littlefield, 1959.

607. Cuthbert, Marion V. *Education and Marginality: A Study of the Negro Woman College Graduate.* New York: 1942.

608. Finch, Edith. *Carey Thomas of Bryn Mawr.* New York: Harper and Brothers, 1947.

609. Fletcher, Robert. "The First Coeds." *American Scholar 7* (1938): 78-93.

610. Frankfort, Roberta. *Collegiate Women: Domesticity and Career in Turn-of-the-Century America.* New York: New York University Press, 1977.

611. Furniss, W. Todd and Graham, Patricia Albjerg, eds. *Women in Higher Education.* Washington, DC: American Council on Education, 1974.

612. Glick, Paul and Parke, Robert Jr. "New Approaches in Studying the Life Cycle of the Family." *Demography 2* (1965): 187-202.

613. Goodsell, Willystine. *Pioneers of Women's Education in the United States.* New York: McGraw-Hill, 1931.

614. Gordon, Lynn D. "Co-Education on Two Campuses: Berkeley and Chicago, 1890-1912." In Mary Kelley, ed., *Woman's Being, Woman's Place: Female Identity and Vocation in American History*, pp. 171-193. Boston: G.K. Hall, 1979.

615. ———. "Annie Nathan Meyer and Barnard College: Mission and Identity in Women's Higher Education, 1889-1950." *History of Education Quarterly 26* (1986): 503-522.

616. Gordon, Sarah H. "Smith College Students: The First Ten Classes, 1879-1888." *History of Education Quarterly 15* (1975): 147-167.

617.   Graham, Patricia Albjerg. *Community and Class in American Education, 1865-1918*. New York: Wiley, 1974.

618.   ———. "Expansion and Exclusion: A History of Women in American Higher Education." *Signs: Journal of Women in Culture and Society 3* (1978): 759-753.

619.   Greene, Maxine. "Honorable Work and Delayed Awakenings: Education and American Women." *Phi Delta Kappan 58* (1976): 25-30.

620.   Guy-Sheftall, Beverly. "Black Women and Higher Education: Spellman and Bennett Colleges Revisited." *Journal of Negro Education 51* (1982): 278-287.

621.   Hague, Amy. "'What If the Power Does Lie Within Me?' Women Students at the University of Wisconsin, 1875-1900." *History of Higher Education Annual* (1984): 78-100.

622.   Haines, Patricia Foster. "For Honor and Alma Mater: Perspectives on Coeducation at Cornell University, 1868-1885." *Journal of Education 159* (1977): 25-37.

623.   ———. "Coeducation and the Development of Leadership Skills in Women: Historical Perspectives from Cornell." In Sari Knopp Biklen and Marilyn B. Brannigan, eds., *Women and Educational Leadership*, pp. 113-128. Lexington, MA: Heath, 1980.

624.   Hareven, Tamara K. "The Family Process: The Historical Study of the Family Life Cycle." *Journal of Social History 7* (1973-1974): 322-329.

625.   Harris, Barbara J. "Recent Work on the History of the Family: A Review Article." *Feminist Studies 3* (1976): 159-172.

626.   Henle, Ellen and Merrill, Marlene. "Antebellum Black Coeds at Oberlin College." *Women's Studies Newsletter 7* (1979): 10.

627.   Hogeland, Ronald W. "Coeducation of the Sexes at Oberlin College: A Study of Social Ideas in Mid-Nineteenth

Century America." *Journal of Social History 6* (1972): 160-176.

628. Horowitz, Helen Lefkowitz. *Alma Mater: Design and Experience in the Women's Colleges from their Nineteenth-Century Beginnings to the 1930's.* New York: Alfred A. Knopf, 1984.

629. Howe, Florence. "Why Educate Women? The Responses of Wellesley and Stanford." In *Myths of Coeducation–Selected Essays, 1964-1983,* pp. 259-269. Bloomington, IN: Indiana University Press, 1984.

630. Hughes, Robert M. and Turner, Joseph A. "Notes on the Higher Education of Women in Virginia." *William and Mary College Quarterly 9* (1929): 325-334.

631. Jones, Thomas Jesse. *Negro Education: A Study of the Private and Higher Schools for Colored People in the United States.* Bureau of Education, Bulletin no. 38, 1916.

632. Kerber, Linda K. "'Why Should Girls Be Learn'd and Wise?': Two Centuries of Higher Education for Women as Seen Through the Unfinished Work of Alice Mary Baldwin." In John Mack Faragher and Florence Howe, eds., *Women and Higher Education in American History,* pp. 18-42. New York: W. W. Norton, 1988.

633. Kohlstedt, Sally Gregory. "Single-Sex Education and Leadership: The Early Years of Simmons College." In Sari Knopp Biklen and Marilyn B. Brannigan, eds., *Women and Educational Leadership,* pp. 93-112. Lexington, MA: Heath, 1980.

634. Lansing, John B. and Kish, Leslie. "Family Life Cycle as an Independent Variable." *American Sociological Review 22* (1957): 512-519.

635. McGuigan, Dorothy Gies. *A Dangerous Experiment: 100 Years of Women at the University of Michigan.* Ann Arbor: Center for Continuing Education of Women, 1970.

636.   Newcomer, Mabel. *A Century of Higher Education for American Women.* New York: Harper and Brothers, 1959.

637.   Noble, Jeanne. *The Negro Woman's College Education.* New York: Bureau of Publications, Teachers College, Columbia University, 1958.

638.   ———. "The Higher Education of Black Women in the Twentieth Century." In John Mack Faragher and Florence Howe, eds., *Women and Higher Education in American History*, pp. 87-106. New York: W. W. Norton, 1988.

639.   Oates, Mary J. and Williamson, Susan. "Women's Colleges and Women Achievers." *Signs: Journal of Women in Culture and Society 3* (1978): 795-806.

640.   Palmieri, Patricia A. "Patterns of Achievement of Single Academic Women at Wellesley College, 1880-1920." *Frontiers 5* (1980): 63-67.

641.   ———. *In Adamless Eden: A Social Portrait of the Academic Community at Wellesley College, 1875-1920.* (Ed.D. thesis, Harvard Graduate School of Education), 1981.

642.   ———. "Here Was Fellowship: A Social Portrait of Academic Women at Wellesley College, 1895-1920." *History of Education Quarterly 23* (1983): 195-214.

643.   ———. "Incipit Vita Nuova: Founding Ideals of the Wellesley College Community." *History of Higher Education Annual* (1983): 59-78.

644.   Richardson, Eudora R. "The Case for the Women's Colleges in the South." *Southern Atlantic Quarterly 29* (1930): 126-139.

645.   Riesman, David. "Continuities and Discontinuities in Women's Education." Bennington College Commencement Address, 1956.

646.   Rosenberg, Rosalind. "The Limits of Access: The History of Coeducation in America." In John Mack Faragher and

Florence Howe, eds., *Women and Higher Education in American History*, pp. 107-129. New York: W. W. Norton, 1988.

647. Rudolph, Frederick. "The Education of Women." In *The American College and University: A History*, pp. 307-328. New York: Alfred A. Knopf, 1962.

648. Rury, John and Harper, Glenn. "The Trouble with Coeducation: Mann and Women at Antioch, 1853-1860." *History of Education Quarterly 26* (1986): 481-502.

649. Sack, Saul. "The Higher Education of Women in Pennsylvania." *Pennsylvania Magazine of History and Biography 83* (1959): 29-73.

650. Seelye, Laurenius Clarke. *The Early History of Smith College, 1871-1910*. Boston: Houghton Mifflin, 1923.

651. Sewall, May Wright. *Domestic and Social Effects of the Higher Education of Women*. c. 1887.

652. Sherzer, Jane. "The Higher Education of Women in the Ohio Valley." *Ohio Historical Quarterly 25* (1916): 1-26.

653. Sicherman, Barbara. "College and Careers: Historical Perspectives on the Lives and Work Patterns of Women College Graduates." In John Mack Faragher and Florence Howe, eds., *Women and Education in American History*, pp. 130-165. New York: W. W. Norton, 1988.

654. Simmons, Adele. "Education and Ideology in Nineteenth-Century America: The Response of Educational Institutions to the Changing Role of Women." In Bernice A. Carroll, ed., *Liberating Women's History: Theoretical and Critical Essays*, pp. 115-126. Urbana: University of Illinois Press, 1976.

655. Slowe, Lucy. "Higher Education for Negro Women." *Journal of Negro Education 2* (1933): 352-358.

656. Solomon, Barbara. *In the Company of Educated Women: A History of Women and Higher Education in America*. New Haven: Yale University Press, 1985.

657. Talbot, Marion. *The Education of Women.* Chicago: University of Chicago Press, 1910.

658. Taylor, James Monroe. *Before Vassar Opened: A Contribution to the History of Higher Education in America.* Boston: Houghton Mifflin, 1914.

659. Terrell, Mary Church. *A Colored Woman in a White World.* Washington, DC: National Association of Colored Women's Clubs, 1968.

660. Tidball, M. Elizabeth. "Perspectives on Academic Women and Affirmative Action." *Educational Record 54* (1973): 130-135.

661. ———. "The Search for Talented Women." *Change 6* (1974): 51-52.

662. ———. "Women's Colleges and Women Achievers Revisited." *Signs: Journal of Women in Culture and Society 5* (1980): 504-517.

663. Uhlenberg, Peter R. "A Study of Cohort Life Cycles: Cohorts of Native-Born Massachusetts Women, 1830-1920." *Journal of Economic History 22* (1972): 184-213.

664. Vinovskis, Maris A. and Richard M. Bernard. "Beyond Catharine Beecher: Female Education in the Antebellum Period." *Signs: Journal of Women in Culture and Society 3* (1978): 856-869.

665. Wein, Roberta. "Women's Colleges and Domesticity, 1875-1918." *History of Education Quarterly 14* (1974): 31-47.

666. Wells, Robert V. "Demographic Change and the Life Cycle of American Families." *Journal of Interdisciplinary History 2* (1971): 273-282.

667. Zimmerman, Joan. "Daughters of Main Street: Culture and the Female Community at Grinnell, 1184-1912." In Mary Kelley, ed., *Woman's Being, Woman's Place: Female Identity and Vocation in American History*, pp. 154-170. Boston: G. K. Hall, 1979.

PART III

WOMEN MAKING HISTORY IN EDUCATION

PART III

WOMEN MAKING HISTORY IN EDUCATION

*A woman is nobody. A wife is everything. A pretty
girl is equal to ten thousand men, and a mother is, next to
God, all powerful. . . . The ladies of Philadelphia . . . are
resolved to maintain their rights as Wives, Belles, Virgins,
and Mothers, and not as Women.*

—*Editorial in the Philadelphia
Ledger and Daily Transcript, 1848*

Introduction

The first Women's Rights Convention was held in a Methodist
chapel in the small town of Seneca Falls, New York in 1848. Three
hundred people, including forty men, gathered to hear Elizabeth Cady
Stanton, Lucretia Mott and a number of other "rebellious" women
begin the process that would, seventy-two years later, finally result in
women obtaining full franchise in the public sphere of government.
Many thought that the boundary between male and female spheres
was permanently breached. Now, however, after nearly another
seventy-two years, the question of woman's "place" threatens to
become an issue again, this time not in terms of political or economic
status, but in terms of the family. While women have achieved at
least minimal access to every area of public life, the nation's children
are suffering—for if the division between public and private, male and
female spheres, has been breached, it has not been eliminated.
Indeed, as women have left home to go to school and to work, men
have not assumed equal responsibility at home. Rather, women
continue to bear the major *social* responsibility for household work
and child care. Our institutions still do not, in any meaningful way,
have policies that support family life, either in government or in the
workplace; the divorce rate is high; rape is increasing; and children
are hungry, both for food and for attention.

Many in the United States, including many women, still
subscribe to the belief that if women "stayed at home" while men
worked, these problems would be solved. In other words, they still
conceive of the world as divided into two, almost mutually exclusive,
areas of social life. This belief, although no longer articulated as it
was by the editorial writer cited above, has not been fundamentally
altered in the social consciousness. Critics argue that an alternative

to the idea of separate spheres can be found in an emphasis on the autonomy of all individuals to freely participate in all areas of social life, including what Martin calls the *productive* and *reproductive* processes of society (799). In her view, these processes are not bifurcated, but occur in all areas of economic, political, and social life—economics as well as the family, politics as well as the church, and particularly in education where the needs of human beings and the needs of the society are most visibly intertwined.

Yet, the conceptual division of social life into rational and emotional, ordered and disordered, public and private continues. In this regard, Maxine Greene writes movingly about the realities of contemporary life:

> In any case, at the present moment, a management ideal (or a game-player paradigm) frequently absorbs and distorts the value of autonomy. As compassion and social concern seem to diminish in the public domain, women's rights are being eroded on all sides: the right to choose, where abortions are concerned; the "welfare mother's" rights to health care and child care; the right to affirmative action in hiring. Insistent talk of "family protection" threatens a new effort to thrust women back into the private sphere. Economic stringencies are affecting equity efforts in the domains of schooling, as federal resources diminish and school systems do less to compensate for longstanding discrimination in classrooms, as they do less to correct the unfairness to females inherent in sex-biased schoolbooks and sexist language. Meanwhile, access to private colleges and universities is being curtailed because of the absence of loans and other supports; and there are fewer and fewer opportunities, therefore, for young women to attempt recently opened ladders to high status in the professions, the arts, and the sciences (671, p. 37).

This section of the bibliography introduces the reader to the history of the separation of public and private life with respect to ideas about women's "fundamental" nature, male and female roles, and the critique of these ideas. It is presented here as a foundation for the study of the search for equity that has been so much a part of modern life in the past twenty-five years.

BIBLIOGRAPHY

668.   Beardsley, Elizabeth. "Traits and Genderization." In Mary
       Vetterling-Bragin, F. A. Elliston and Jane English, eds.,
       Feminism and Philosophy, pp. 117-123. Totowa, NJ:
       Littlefield, 1977.

669.   Chafetz, J. S. *Masculine, Feminine or Human?* Itasca, IL: F. E.
       Peacock, 1978.

670.   Elshtain, Jean Bethke. *Public Man, Private Woman.*
       Princeton: Princeton University Press, 1981.

671.   Greene, Maxine. "Sex Equity as a Philosophical Problem." In
       Susan S. Klein, ed., *Handbook for Achieving Sex Equity
       Through Education*, pp. 29-43. Baltimore: Johns Hopkins
       University Press, 1985.

672.   Janeway Elizabeth. *Man's World, Woman's Place.* New York:
       William Morrow, 1971.

673.   Lowe, Marian and Hubbard, Ruth, eds. *Women's Nature:
       Rationalizations of Inequality.* Elmsford, NY: Pergamon,
       1983.

674.   Moulton, Janice. "The Myth of the Neutral 'Man'." In Mary
       Vetterling-Braggin, F. A. Elliston and Jane English, eds.,
       Feminism and Philosophy, pp. 124-137. Totowa, NJ:
       Littlefield, Adams, 1977.

675.   Rosenberg, Rosalind. "In Search of Women's Nature, 1850-
       1920." *Feminist Studies 3* (Fall 1975): 141-154.

676.   Rossi, Alice S. "Sex Equality: The Beginnings of Ideology." In
       Elizabeth S. Maccia et al., eds., *Women and Education*,
       pp. 313-327. Springfield, IL: Thomas, 1975.

677.   ———. "Equality Between the Sexes: An Immodest Proposal."
       Daedalus 117 (1988): 25-71.

678.   Rothman, Sheila. *Woman's Proper Place: A History of
       Changing Ideals and Practices, 1870 to the Present.* New
       York: Basic Books, 1978.

679.   Rowbotham, Sheila. *Women's Consciousness, Man's World.*
        Harmondsworth, Middlesex: Penguin Books, 1974.

680.   Smith, Dorothy E. "A Peculiar Eclipsing: Women's Exclusion
        from Man's Culture." In Renate D. Klein and Deborah
        Lynn Steinberg, eds., *Radical Voices: A Decade of
        Feminist Resistance*, pp. 3-21. New York: Pergamon
        Press, 1989.

681.   Warren, M. A. *The Nature of Woman: An Encyclopedia and
        Guide to the Literature.* Inverness, CA: Edgepress, 1980.

CHAPTER 7

The Search for Equity in Education

*If university education means anything beyond the
processing of human beings into expected roles, through
credit hours, tests, and grades . . . it implies an ethical
and intellectual contract between teacher and student.
This contract must remain intuitive, dynamic, unwritten;
but we must turn to it again and again if learning is to be
reclaimed from the depersonalizing and cheapening
pressures of the present-day academic scene.*
                                                —*Adrienne Rich, 1977*

When the poet and essayist Adrienne Rich spoke the words
quoted above to a convocation at Douglass College, she was exhorting
the women in her audience to *claim* an education for themselves
rather than simply *receiving* one (805, p. 231). At the heart of her
message was a belief that it was not enough for women to be
"admitted" to higher education, "admitted" to the professions,
"admitted" to public life. Rather, for Rich, education in the canon of
a male-defined liberal arts curriculum in schools where women were
only a fraction of the faculty was insufficient. The "most significant
fact for you," she said,

> is that what you learn here, the very texts you read, the
> lectures you hear, the way your studies are divided into
> categories and fragmented one from the other—all this
> reflects, to a very large degree, neither objective reality,
> nor an accurate picture of the past, nor a group of
> rigorously tested observations about human behavior.
> What you can learn here (and I mean not only at
> Douglass but any college in any university) is how *men*
> have perceived and organized their experience, their
> history, their ideas of social relationships, good and evil,
> sickness and health, etc. When you read or hear about
> "great issues," "major texts," "the mainstream of
> Western thought," you are hearing about what men,
> above all white men, in their male subjectivity, have
> decided is important (805, p. 232).

151

This belief, of course, was not a new one. What *was* new was a cadre of women who, in the late 1960s and early 1970s set about to do something about it. Scholars in a variety of disciplines—the sciences, the humanities, the arts, and the professions—began to create a field of study called Women's Studies, the purpose of which was to reclaim, rediscover, and reconceptualize the body of knowledge we call "Western thought." While most identified themselves as feminist, and sought as a part of their personal and professional lives to improve the equity and quality of women's and men's lives in a variety of ways, their intellectual work focused on the problem of how to "re-vision" (874) the knowledge base that underlay social thought. To do this, they adopted the view that knowledge should be understood and interpreted from the perspective of women's experience.

Women's Studies scholars provided the impetus, the scholarship, and the theory that launched a new search for equity, not in law this time, but in education. From that search developed not only a viable new field of study, but also a political and social effort to reform higher education and schooling in terms of curriculum and pedagogy as well as in terms of new research questions for the disciplines. From that search also developed the theoretical bases of a revised social view of the world, and for a redefinition of the meaning of education, of what it means to be an educated person.

The Development of Women's Studies

The first Women's Studies Program was established at San Diego State College in California in 1970. By the early 1980s, there were about 350 undergraduate and graduate programs which offered certificates, majors, and masters degrees and thousands of individual courses that focused on women and their experience. Most Women's Studies programs were housed in arts and sciences departments and schools, but women and men in professional and technical schools also researched issues pertaining to women and taught Women's Studies courses.

At the center of the Women's Studies program is an interdisciplinary focus that cuts across artificially fragmented knowledge areas and utilizes pedagogical methods designed to empower and give "voice" to those, women and men, who have not been represented in "mainstream" academic thought. Thus, Women's Studies scholars have laid part of the groundwork for current interest in the impact of cultural and other forms of diversity on teaching and learning. At the center of Women's Studies courses is an assumption that the *person* rather than the event, or theory, or equation is at the heart of the matter. Thus, Women's Studies scholarship and teaching may ask fundamentally different questions about the world and its activities. These questions fall into several categories. At the most basic, they ask "What were women doing during this period?" and "How did this event affect women?" From these kinds of questions has come the realization that, in fact, women's experience has often been significantly different from men's. Joan Kelly's question, "Did Women Have a Renaissance?" (081), for example, produced the understanding that the "great leap forward" in human expression and liberty from an all-encompassing church did not appreciably apply to women. Indeed, Kelly asserts that "the startling fact is that women as a group, especially among the classes that dominated Italian urban life, experienced a contraction of social and personal options that men of their classes either did not, as was the case with the bourgeoisie, or did not experience as markedly, as was the case with the nobility" (081, p. 20).

A second set of questions, somewhat more complex, focuses on such issues as "What was the reaction of women to the circumstances in which they found themselves?" Part of the complexity of this kind of question is that women's reactions were often as, or more, diverse as the reactions of men to any particular idea or event. Furthermore, because women have largely been socialized to believe that they are weaker, or lesser, or, at any rate, *different* from men, and that they either should not be concerned with "major" issues or cannot be expected to understand or contribute their own perspective to a problem, a large majority of women simply accede to prevailing assumptions and stereotypical thinking about themselves. Several interesting results have come from this kind of question. First, awareness has grown that in many ways there is greater diversity *within* the class called "woman" than there is between women and men. This awareness has caused a considerable amount of trouble in Women's Studies, because the *political* agenda of many Women's Studies scholars appears to require a solidarity that frequently does not exist. Second, when teaching Women's Studies courses, it is often necessary to invest a certain amount of time in what has come to be called "consciousness-raising" to encourage women to the point where they can comfortably ask questions about normative ideas. It is difficult, for example, for many women to believe that if a woman is raped she did not in some way "ask for it." Similarly, it is hard for many women to understand that the lack of women in leadership positions in business and the professions is probably not either natural or accidental. Third, asking this sort of question has led to the discovery of great numbers of previously unknown women whose reactions to events were proactive rather than reactive, and whose contributions, although largely forgotten, are impressive. The sociologist Charlotte Perkins Gilman for example, writing at the turn of the century in language that sounds as current as yesterday's editorial columns, had a great deal to say about what Betty Friedan, apparently ignorant of Gilman's work, later called "the feminine mystique" (281).

A third and even more complex set of questions systematically emerging from Women's Studies asks "How can women's experience be used to analyze and interpret disciplinary knowledge?" and "What would be the possible effects of a woman's perspective on social life?" Taking as a basic tenet that "the personal is political," Women's Studies scholars and activists began to examine ways in which their perspective could act to transform not only the academic disciplines, but the very society itself. Here, the wide variety of feminist theoretical perspectives begins to make a difference in interpretations and recommendations. Donovan (686), for example, analyzes several different theoretical positions with respect to a "feminist" view of the world that range from an insistence on the common humanity—and therefore, equality—of men and women to an equally strong insistence that women, by virtue of their experience, are possessed of a particularly useful set of knowledge and skills that would be of immeasurable benefit to the society if adopted. These differences in perspective lead to very different answers to social and educational policy questions. Should women obtain access to the physical sciences as they are presently constituted or should they act to alter the very *program* of the sciences (871, 881, 882)? Should women have particular protections in the workplace in terms of safety and particular rights to take maternity and family emergency leaves or should they take the workplace as men find it? Should women be required to choose whether or not they will participate in public life (if such a choice is, indeed, open to them), or should the nature of individual responsibilities in social life be reconceptualized? These kinds of questions have resulted in a set of critiques that constitute one of the most important debates not only in Women's Studies, but in American life.

Taken together, the questions raised by Women's Studies scholars and activists form the basis for the search for equity in education, which is viewed by nearly all as central to the redesign of the lives of women and men. It is perhaps too early to tell whether Women's Studies will succeed in making a permanent impact on the life of the university or the school: evidence in this regard is mixed. Yet, the issues raised by Women's Studies scholars have become part of the debate on public policy in the broader society, and the transformation of knowledge in terms of gender and culture is clearly underway. It is possible that the result will be, in fact, a redefinition of what it means to be an educated person.

The Search for Equity in Higher Education

Fueled, in part, by the development of Women's Studies, the search for equity in higher education over the past two decades has been an effort to build upon and extend the work of 19th and early 20th century women who created a place for women in higher education. Some of the issues have been similar to those of an earlier era: for example, Conway has strongly asserted that the education of women in single-sex institutions is by far the best way to ensure that they receive a quality education (685). In her view, the rise of coeducational institutions since Oberlin began admitting women in the 1830s has resulted in a decline in women's access to all areas of education and a continuing emphasis on educating women to secondary status in society (685). Others argue that women in coeducational institutions, especially in the social sciences, have had a significant influence on social thought, particularly in the area of research on sex differences and socialization to social role (569).

Many issues in the contemporary search for equity in higher education are relatively new ones. For example, a significant amount of work has been devoted to the status of women in academe—something that has become a "problem" only since women began to obtain higher educations in large numbers. Patricia Graham argues that the emergence of the major research university has had a negative impact on women academics (618). This occurred in three ways. First, women had historically been excluded from the universities setting the research standards; second, the requirements for professional scholarship were increasingly antithetical to social norms of feminine behavior; and, third, the academic areas and types of colleges in which women had gained acceptance were lower in status and prestige (169). Indeed, it is a matter of record that more women were participating in academic life in the 1930s than in the 1970s (618).

Other areas in which the search for equity has proceeded is in developing a research agenda for women's experience in higher education that includes women of color and women from working class backgrounds (704, 711), the experience of women as doctoral students (706, 710), and the role of higher education in developing a sense of identity in women (708, 712). In addition, an enormous amount of work has been done on the transformation of curriculum and pedagogy (much of which will be discussed in the next chapter), on the institutionalization of affirmative action programs in higher education, and on issues of sexual harassment (705).

Because the literature on equity issues in higher education is perhaps more extensive than the contemporary literature on any other aspect of women's education, it is too large to give here except in abbreviated form. Thus the bibliography for this section is intended to provide the reader with a sampling of work which raises the major issues in the field rather than offering a complete selection of citations.

The Search for Equity in Schooling

Much of the research and scholarship on equity in higher education has concerned reconceptualizing the very nature of collegiate experience and laying the theoretical ground work for change. In contrast, the search for equity in schooling has emphasized practice. In part, this can be viewed as a reflection of the differences between arts and sciences disciplines and professional schools. Biklen and Shakeshaft, for example, argue that theoretical development in education has lagged behind other fields for a number of reasons. First, education is a multidisciplinary pursuit that draws from other areas of knowledge. Second, education traditionally has been perceived as secondary to the arts and sciences disciplines, or as a field of study interested only in "method." Third, and perhaps most important, teacher educators—like all educators in professional areas—have a different set of problems, particularly the needs of schools. They write:

> Educational practices have so often lacked sex equity
> that many educational researchers and activists felt it
> imperative to focus on applied areas. Curricula,
> practices, and structures that perpetuate discrimination
> have absorbed our attention rather than the more
> theoretical, less practical concerns. Motivated by a
> desire to change these practices for the next generation,
> women's studies practitioners in education have focused
> on schools (934, p. 50).

Concerns about equity in schools focus on a number of areas, including bias in the curriculum, in student-teacher interaction, in school sex role socialization practices, and in the employment structure of schools that enables men to manage and women to teach (979, 982). The work of the Sadkers (762, 763, 764) is illustrative in this regard. They have found particular bias in differential treatment received by boys and girls in schools, both academically and socially. Girls receive less praise for good academic work and more for neatness; they are more often the "helpers" in the classroom; they receive less actual teacher attention; and they are less likely to be identified as potential achievers in math and science as well as less likely to be identified as learning disabled. In short, academically as well as socially, girls are still routinely being educated in traditional "feminine" understandings for roles as homemakers and prevented from acquiring the knowledge that is thought to be of the most worth in the society. At the same time, girls as well as boys are receiving very little instruction in the skills required for family life.

The search for equity in schooling, like its counterpart in higher education, is a long-term process that is only in its initial stages. Indeed, equity issues of all kinds have been submerged in recent years with another round of insistence on "excellence," by which is generally meant the internalization of and adherence to traditional male-defined subject matter. Nor has the public assumed any particular responsibility for equity issues in terms of a real debate in areas of educational policy. Shakeshaft summarizes the problem when she writes:

> As troubling as it is to hear political and educational leaders falsely blaming the mediocrity of the school system on those who seek a system that offers women, people of color, and handicapped students a fair shake, it is even more disturbing to chart the failure of the public to see the reliance of excellence on equity. At best, the two are described as "twin goals"; at worst, the importance of equitable practices to excellence in education is flatly denied. By failing to articulate the relationship of equity to excellence or by perpetuating the myth that the two are unrelated . . . we make it easier to disregard equity as a national concern (924, p. 499).

If arguments for the inclusion of girls in the common school in the 19th century were largely centered on the need to provide better mothers for the nation, contemporary arguments for equity for girls center on the need to provide the nation with an employable workforce that will increasingly be composed of women. Unfortunately, schooling in the United States attempts to be "gender-blind" while maintaining gender-biased practices as a matter of course. What has emerged in recent years, however, is the beginning of a discussion on what it means to be an educated person, and it is to that discussion that we can now turn our attention.

Redefining the Educated Woman

From the work of a small group of feminist educators has come, quite recently, a redefinition of the educated woman that is designed to alter the definition of education and its outcomes (778, 780, 785, 787, 789, 799, 802, 805). While small in number, this group has produced a body of thought that does not stop at the desire for mere equity, if equity is taken to mean access to existing education theory and institutions. Rather, from a variety of perspectives, they claim that women, by virtue of their socialization and experience, have developed a different *voice* and that this voice has exceptional merit for conditions at the end of the 20th century.

Asserting that women's knowledge, experience, and moral sense have been left out of the development of social thought, they describe the conditions of that exclusion as harmful not only to women but to men as well. For women, it means that they will be "forced into male molds" (794, p. 147) and deprived of the ability to use their own voices (778). The question also arises as to whether or not male norms are particularly good for men (794, p. 147). In addition, Martin argues that the very definition of an educated person is constrained by the limitation of male-dominated analytic models because they "divorce . . . mind from body, thought from action, and reason from feeling and emotion" (794, p. 147). Rather, these women argue that an adequate ideal of the educated person must combine these elements.

Of particular interest in this work is Martin's distinction between the *productive* and *reproductive* processes of society. Productive processes, she argues, are those that are concerned with economic, political, and artistic life. Reproductive processes involve caretaking—the bearing and raising of children, the care of the sick, the care of the old, the care of the unstable. Both, she argues, are fundamentally necessary to a flourishing society (799). To the extent that formal education addresses only the productive processes, it provides rationale and substance for only one definition of education and one approach to solving the problems of the society.

Relying on women's traditional roles as the basis for a relational, inclusive, and flexible approach to social life and social problems, all these scholars reject the notion that women are either inferior to men or superior only in their own sphere—the family. Furthermore, they argue that if this approach were taken seriously, we could perhaps begin to find some solutions to the problems that

increasingly plague us, including the protection and care of the planet
we live on.

Thus, at the present time, the search for equity in education
has led its explorers to a reconceptualized vision of education itself.
Whether or not such a vision will make significant inroads into
educational thought, unfortunately, may depend more on the
conditions of life in which we find ourselves than on the eagerness of
traditional scholars to look with interest on this new work. Indeed, it
may be that, as a society, we have to become a great deal worse off
before we will be willing to undertake a careful examination of
solutions emanating from nontraditional sources such as these.

BIBLIOGRAPHY

The Development of Women's Studies

682.   Bowles, G. and Duelli-Klein, R. *Theories of Women's Studies.*
        London: Routledge and Kegan Paul, 1983.

683.   Boxer, Marilyn J. "For and About Women: The Theory and
        Practice of Women's Studies in the United States." In E.
        Minnich, J. O'Barr, and R. Rosenfeld, eds.,
        Reconstructing the Academy, pp. 69-103. Chicago:
        University of Chicago Press, 1988.

684.   Conway, Jill K. "Coeducation and Women's Studies: Two
        Approaches to the Question of Woman's Place in the
        Contemporary University." *Daedalus 103* (1974): 239-249.

685.   De Lauretis, Teresa, ed. *Feminist Studies/Critical Studies.*
        Milwaukee, WI: Center for Twentieth Century Studies,
        University of Wisconsin, 1986.

686.   Donovan, Josephine. *Feminist Theory: The Intellectual
        Traditions of American Feminism.* New York: Frederick
        Unger, 1988.

687.   Fausto-Sterling, Anne. "Women's Studies and Science."
        Women's Studies Quarterly 8 (1984): 4-7.

688.   Jones, Lillian H. "Ethnic and Women's Studies: An Attempt
        at Educating the Academy." *Radical Teacher 37* (1990):
        27-29.

689.   Klein, Renate D. "The 'Men-Problem' in Women's Studies:
       The Expert, the Ignoramus and the Poor Dear." In
       Renate D. Klein and Deborah Lynn Steinberg, eds.,
       Radical Voices: A Decade of Feminist Resistance, pp.
       106-120. New York: Pergamon Press, 1989.

690.   Leffler, A., Gillespie, D., and Ratner, E. "Academic Feminists
       and the Women's Movement." *Ain't I a Woman? 4* (1973).

691.   Lerner, Gerda. "On the Teaching and Organization of
       Feminist Studies." In Rae Lee Spiorin, ed., *Female
       Studies V*, pp. 34-37. Pittsburgh: KNOW, Inc., 1972.

692.   MacKinnon, Catherine. "Feminism, Marxism, Method, and
       the State: An Agenda for Theory." *Signs: Journal of
       Women in Culture and Society 7* (1982): 515-44.

693.   Marks, Elaine. "Deconstructing in Women's Studies to
       Reconstructing the Humanities." In Marilyn R. Schuster
       and Susan R. Van Dyne, eds., *Women's Place in the
       Academy*, pp. 172-187. Totowa, NJ: Rowman and
       Allenheld, 1985.

694.   Minnich, Elizabeth, O'Barr, Jean, and Rosenfeld, Rachel, eds.
       *Reconstructing the Academy: Women's Education and
       Women's Studies.* Chicago: University of Chicago Press,
       1988.

695.   National Council for Research on Women. *Mainstreaming
       Minority Women's Studies Programs.* New York:
       National Council for Research on Women, 1989.

696.   Rosenberg, Rosalind. "The Academic Prism: The New View of
       American Women." In Carol Ruth Berkin and Mary Beth
       Norton, eds., *Women of America: A History*, pp. 318-41.
       Boston: Houghton Mifflin, 1979.

697.   Schramm, S. S. "Do It Yourself: Women's Studies." In S. S.
       Schramm, ed., *Female Studies VIII*, pp. 1-4. Pittsburgh:
       KNOW, Inc., 1975.

698.   Sicherman, Barbara. "The Invisible Woman: The Case for
       Women's Studies." In W. Todd Furniss and Patricia
       Albjerg Graham, eds., *Women in Higher Education*, pp.

155-177. Washington, DC: American Council on Education, 1974.

699. Tobias, Sheila. "Teaching Female Studies: Looking Back Over Three Years." In Elizabeth S. Maccia et al., eds., *Women and Education*, pp. 282-289. Springfield, IL: Thomas, 1975.

700. Zinn, Maxine Baca et al. "The Costs of Exclusionary Practices in Women's Studies." In E. Minnich, J. O'Barr, and R. Rosenfeld, eds., *Reconstructing the Academy*, pp. 125-138. Chicago: University of Chicago Press, 1988.

The Search for Equity in Higher Education

701. Bogart, K. *Towards Equity in Academe: An Action Manual.* Washington, DC: Project on the Status and Education of Women, Association of American Colleges, 1984.

702. Cless, Elizabeth L. "A Modest Proposal for the Educating of Women." *American Scholar 38* (1969): 618-627.

703. Clifford, Geraldine Joncich. "'Shaking Dangerous Questions from the Crease': Gender and American Higher Education." *Feminist Issues 3* (1983): 3-61.

704. Fleming, Jacqueline. "Black Women in Black and White College Environments: The Making of a Matriarch." *Journal of Social Issues 39* (1983).

705. Hall, R. and Sandler, B. R. *The Classroom Climate: A Chilly One For Women?* Washington, DC: Project on the Status and Education of Women, Association of American Colleges, 1982.

706. Hanson, Marjorie. "Reflections of a Stranger in a Strange Land." *Educational Horizons 64* (1986): 140-141.

707. Kirschner, Susan, Atkinson, Jane, and Arch, Elizabeth. "Reassessing Coeducation." In Marilyn R. Schuster and Susan R. Van Dyne, eds., *Women's Place in the Academy*, pp. 30-47. Totowa, NJ: Rowman and Allenheld, 1985.

708.   Komarovsky, Mirra. *Women in College: Shaping New
        Feminine Identities.* New York: Basic Books, 1985.

709.   Langland, Elizabeth and Gove, Walter, eds. *A Feminist
        Perspective in the Academy: The Difference It Makes.*
        Chicago: University of Chicago Press, 1981.

710.   Lincoln, Yvonna S. "The Ladder and the Leap." *Educational
        Horizons 64* (1986): 113-116.

711.   Middleton, Lorenzo and Roark, A. C. "Lonely Social Life of
        Black Women on White Campus." *Chronicle of Higher
        Education 22* (July 20, 1981).

712.   Perun, Pamela J., ed. *The Undergraduate Woman: Issues in
        Educational Equity.* Lexington, MA: Heath, 1982.

713.   ――― and Giele, Janet Z. "Life after College: Historical Links
        between Women's Education and Women's Work." In
        Pamela J. Perun, ed., *The Undergraduate Woman: Issues
        in Educational Equity*, pp. 375-398. Lexington, MA: D. C.
        Heath, 1982.

714.   Pitman, Mary Anne. "Continuing Education for Women—
        CHECKMATE?" *Educational Horizons 64* (1986):
        123-126.

715.   Salner, Marcia. "Women, Graduate Education, and Feminist
        Knowledge." *Journal of Education 167* (1985): 46-58.

716.   Sandler, Bernice R. "The Quiet Revolution on Campus: How
        Sex Discrimination Has Changed." *Chronicle of Higher
        Education* (February 29, 1984): 72.

717.   Westervelt, Esther Manning. *Women's Higher and Continuing
        Education: An Annotated Bibliography.* New York:
        College Entrance Examination Board, 1971.

The Search for Equity in Schooling

718.   Agre, Gene P. and Finkelstein, Barbara. "Feminism in School
        Reform: The Last Fifteen Years." *Teachers College
        Record 80* (1978): 307-315.

719. Allain, Violet Anselmini. "Women in Education: The Future." *Educational Horizons 60* (1981): 52-56.

720. Arnot, Madeleine, ed. *Gender and the Politics of Schooling.* New York: Hutchinson, 1987.

721. —— and Weiner, Gaby, eds. *Gender Under Scrutiny: New Enquiries in Education.* New York: Hutchinson, 1987.

722. Best, R. *We've All Got Scars: What Boys and Girls Learn in Elementary School.* Bloomington, IN: Indiana University Press, 1983.

723. Bitters, Barbara A. "Sex Equity in Vocational Education." In Anne O'Brien Carelli, ed., *Sex Equity in Education: Readings and Strategies*, pp. 229-247. Springfield, IL: Thomas, 1988.

724. Block, Jeanne H. "Gender Differences and Implications for Educational Policy." *American Psychologist 28* (1978): 512-526.

725. Bornstein, R. *Title IX Compliance and Sex Equity: Definition, Distinctions, Costs and Benefits.* New York: Urban Diversity Series, No. 73. Teachers College, Columbia University, 1981.

726. Broadhurst, Kenneth. "Solving the Exclusion Problem: The Key to Sex Equitable Education in Math, Science, and Technology." In Anne O'Brien Carelli, ed., *Sex Equity in Education: Readings and Strategies*, pp. 145-155. Springfield, IL: Thomas, 1988.

727. Calabrese, Marylyn E. "What Is Sex Fair Education?" In Anne O'Brien Carelli, ed., *Sex Equity in Education: Readings and Strategies*, pp. 75-82. Springfield, IL: Thomas, 1988.

728. Campbell, Patricia B. and Susan S. Klein. "Equity Issues in Education." In *Encyclopedia of Educational Research, 5th ed.* New York: Macmillan, 1982.

729.   Carelli, Anne O'Brien. "Introduction." In Anne O'Brien
        Carelli, ed., *Sex Equity in Education: Readings and
        Strategies*, pp. xi-xxii. Springfield, IL: Thomas, 1988.

730.   ——. "What is Title XI?" and "Federal Anti-Discrimination
        Laws Pertaining to Schools." In *Sex Equity in Education:
        Readings and Strategies*, pp. 83-93. Springfield, IL:
        Thomas, 1988.

731.   ——, ed. *Sex Equity in Education: Readings and Strategies*.
        Springfield, IL: Thomas, 1988.

732.   Chafetz, Janet Saltzman. *Gender Equity*. Newbury Park, CA:
        Sage, 1989.

733.   Deem, Rosemary. *Women and Schooling*. London: Routledge
        and Kegan Paul, 1978.

734.   Delamont, Sara. *Sex Roles and the School*. London: Methuen,
        1980.

735.   DeShazer, Mary K. "'To be Educated Themselves': Current
        Feminist Efforts in School Reform." *Educational
        Horizons 60* (1981): 30-35.

736.   Epperson, Sharon E. "Studies Link Subtle Sex Bias in Schools
        with Women's Behavior in the Workplace." *Wall Street
        Journal* (September 16 1988): 19.

737.   Fantini, Mario. "Sexism: A Commitment to Solutions."
        Journal of Teacher Education 26 (1975): 292, 304.

738.   Farmer, Helen and Seliger, J. "Sex Equity in Career and
        Vocational Education." In Susan S. Klein, ed., *Handbook
        for Achieving Sex Equity Through Education*, pp.
        319-359. Baltimore: Johns Hopkins University, 1985.

739.   Frazier, Nancy and Sadker, Myra, eds. *Sexism in School and
        Society*. New York: Harper and Row, 1973.

740.   Geadelmann, Patricia L. "Sex Equity in Physical Education
        and Athletics." In Susan S. Klein, ed., *Handbook for
        Achieving Sex Equity Through Education*, pp. 319-7.
        Baltimore: Johns Hopkins University Press, 1985.

741. Gordon, Barbara J. A. and Addison, Linda. "Gifted Girls and Women in Education." In Susan S. Klein, ed., *Handbook for Achieving Sex Equity through Education*, pp. 391-415. Baltimore: Johns Hopkins University Press, 1985.

742. Hahn, Carole L. and Powers, Jane Bernard. "Sex Equity in Social Studies." In Susan S. Klein, ed., *Handbook for Achieving Sex Equity Through Education*, pp. 280-297. Baltimore: Johns Hopkins University Press, 1985.

743. Harley, Ruth. "Sex-Role Pressures and the Socialization of the Male Child." *Psychological Reports 5* (1959): 457-468.

744. Harvey, Glen. *Competing Interpretations of Equity.* Washington, DC: National Institute of Education, 1982.

745. —— and Noble, Elizabeth. "Economic Considerations for Achieving Sex Equity through Education." In Susan S. Klein, ed., *Handbook for Achieving Sex Equity through Education*, pp. 17-28. Baltimore: Johns Hopkins University Press, 1985.

746. Jacklin, Carol Nagy. "Boys and Girls Entering School." In Michael Marland, ed., *Sex Differentiation and Schooling*, pp. 8-17. London: Heinemann Educational Books, 1983.

747. ——. "Female and Male: Issues of Gender." *American Psychologist 44* (1989): 127-133.

748. Klein, Susan S., ed. *Handbook for Achieving Sex Equity through Education.* Baltimore: Johns Hopkins University Press, 1985.

749. ——, Russo, L. N., Campbell, P., and Harvey, G. "Examining the Achievement of Sex Equity In and Through Education." In Susan S. Klein, ed., *Handbook for Achieving Sex Equity through Education*, pp. 1-11. Baltimore: Johns Hopkins University Press, 1985.

750. —— et al. "Summary and Recommendations for the Continued Achievement of Sex Equity in and through Education." In Susan S. Klein, ed., *Handbook for Achieving Sex Equity through Education*, pp. 489-524. Baltimore: Johns Hopkins University Press, 1985.

751.   ———— and Bogart, Karen. "Implications for Increasing Sex
       Equity at All Educational Levels." *Educational
       Researcher 15* (1986): 20-21.

752.   Lee, Patrick C. and Nancy B. Gropper. "A Cultural Analysis
       of Sex Role in the School." *Journal of Teacher Education
       26* (1975): 335-339.

753.   Lyon, Nancy. "A Report on Children's Toys and Socialization
       to Sex Roles." *Ms. 1* (1972): 57-59, 98.

754.   Maccia, Elizabeth Steiner, ed. *Women and Education.*
       Springfield, IL: Thomas, 1973.

755.   Maehr, M. "On Doing Well in Science: Why Johnny No
       Longer Excels; Why Sarah Never Did." In S. Paris, G.
       Olson, and H. Stephenson, eds., *Learning and Motivation
       in the Classroom*, pp. 179-210. Hillsdale, NJ: Lawrence
       Erlbaum, 1984.

756.   Marland, Michael, ed. *Sex Differentiation and Schooling.*
       London: Heinemann Educational Books, 1983.

757.   ————. "Towards a Programme of Action." In Michael
       Marland, ed., *Sex Differentiation and Schooling*, pp.
       202-213. London: Heinemann Educational Books, 1983.

758.   ————. "School as a Sexist Amplifier." In Michael Marland,
       ed., *Sex Differentiation and Schooling*, pp. 1-7. London:
       Heinemann Educational Books, 1983.

759.   Minuchin, Patricia. "The Schooling of Tomorrow's Women."
       In Elizabeth S. Maccia et al., eds., *Women and
       Education*, pp. 347-356. Springfield, IL: Thomas, 1975.

760.   National Advisory Council on Women's Educational
       Programs. *Title IX: The Half Full, Half Empty Glass.*
       Washington, DC: National Advisory Council on Women's
       Educational Programs, 1981.

761.   Pottker, Janice and Fishel, Andrew, eds. *Sex Bias in the
       Schools.* Cranbury, NJ: Associated University Presses,
       1977.

762. Sadker, Myra Pollack and Sadker, David. *Sex Equity Handbook for Schools*. New York: Longman, 1982.

763. ———. "Sexism in the Schoolroom of the '80s." *Psychology Today 19* (March 1985): 54-57.

764. ——— and Donald, Mary. "Subtle Sexism at School." *Contemporary Education 60* (1989): 204-212.

765. Schau, Candace Garrett, with Carol Kehr Tittle. "Educational Equity and Sex Role Development." In Susan S. Klein, ed., *Handbook for Achieving Sex Equity Through Education*, pp. 78-90. Baltimore: Johns Hopkins University Press, 1985.

766. Schmuck, Patricia A. "Administrative Strategies for Implementing Sex Equity." In Susan S. Klein, ed., *Handbook for Achieving Sex Equity through Education*, pp. 91-94. Baltimore: Johns Hopkins University Press, 1985.

767. ——— et al. "Administrative Strategies for Institutionalizing Sex Equity in Education and the Role of Government." In Susan S. Klein, ed., *Handbook for Achieving Sex Equity through Education*, pp. 95-123. Baltimore: Johns Hopkins University Press, 1985.

768. Spender, Dale. "Education: the Patriarchal Paradigm and the Response to Feminism." In Dale Spender, ed., *Men's Studies Modified*, pp. 155-173. Oxford: Pergamon Press, 1981.

769. Stacey, Judith et al., eds. *And Jill Came Tumbling After: Sexism in American Education*. New York: Dell, 1974.

770. Sutherland, Margaret B. *Sex Bias in Education*. Oxford: Basil Blackwell, 1981.

771. Tetreault, Mary K. and Schmuck, Patricia. "Equity, Educational Reform, and Gender." *Issues in Education 3* (1985): 63.

772. Tittle, Carol Kehr. "Assumptions about the Nature and Value of Sex Equity." In Susan S. Klein, ed., *Handbook for*

Achieving Sex Equity through Education, pp. 13-15.
Baltimore: Johns Hopkins University Press, 1985.

773.   ———. "Gender Research and Education." *American
        Psychologist 41* (1986): 1161-1168.

774.   Truely, Walteen Grady. "The Difference Difference Makes:
        Sex Equity in Urban Schools." In Anne O'Brien Carelli,
        ed., *Sex Equity in Education: Readings and Strategies*,
        pp. 175-186. Springfield, IL: Thomas, 1988.

775.   Weitzman, Lenore. *Sex Role Socialization: A Focus on Women.*
        Palo Alto, CA: Mayfield, 1979.

776.   Yee, Albert H. "Are Schools a Feminized Society?"
        Educational Leadership 31 (1973): 128-133.

Redefining the Educated Woman

777.   As, Berit. "The Feminist University." In Renate D. Klein and
        Deborah Lynn Steinberg, eds., *Radical Voices: A Decade
        of Feminist Resistance*, pp. 192-198. New York: Pergamon
        Press, 1989.

778.   Belenky, M., Clinchy, B., Goldberger, N., and Tarule, J.
        *Women's Ways of Knowing: The Development of Self,
        Voice, and Mind.* New York: Basic Books, 1986.

779.   Chodorow, Nancy. *The Reproduction of Mothering.* Berkeley:
        University of California Press, 1978.

780.   Clinchy, B., Belenky, M., Goldberger, N., and Tarule, J.
        "Connected Education for Women." *Journal of Education
        167* (1985): 28-45.

781.   Ferguson, Ann. "Woman's Moral Voice: Superior, Inferior, or
        Just Different?" In John Mack Faragher and Florence
        Howe, eds., *Women and Higher Education in American
        History*, pp. 183-197. New York: W. W. Norton, 1988.

782.   Gilligan, Carol. "In a Different Voice: Women's Conception of
        the Self and of Morality." *Harvard Educational Review
        47* (1977): 481-517.

783. ———. "Woman's Place in Man's Life Cycle." *Harvard Educational Review 49* (1979): 431-446.

784. ———. "Why Should A Woman Be More Like a Man?" *Psychology Today* (June 1982): 68-77.

785. ———. *In a Different Voice.* Cambridge: Harvard University Press, 1982.

786. Grumet, Madeleine R. "Conception, Contradiction, and Curriculum." *Journal of Curriculum Theorizing 3* (1981): 287-298.

787. ———. *Bitter Milk: Women and Teaching.* Amherst, MA: University of Massachusetts Press, 1988.

788. ———. "Generations: Reconceptualist Curriculum Theory and Teacher Education." *Journal of Teacher Education 40* (1989): 13-17.

789. Kolbenschlag, Madonna. *Lost in the Land of Oz.* New York: Harper and Row, 1988.

790. Martin, Jane Roland. "The Disciplines and the Curriculum." *Educational Theory and Philosophy 1* (1969): 23-40.

791. ———. "What Should We Do with a Hidden Curriculum When We Find One?" *Curriculum Inquiry 6* (1976): 135-151.

792. ———. "The Ideal of the Educated Person." *Educational Theory 31* (1981): 97-109.

793. ———. "Needed: A New Paradigm for Liberal Education." In *Philosophy and Education,* pp. 37-59. Chicago: National Society for the Study of Education, 1981.

794. ———. "Excluding Women from the Educational Realm." *Harvard Educational Review 52* (1982): 133-148.

795. ———. "Two Dogmas of Curriculum." *Synthese 51* (1982): 5-20.

796. ———. "Seeing What Is Missing from Educational Theory and Practice through the Study of Women." Paper read at the

Symposium on the New Scholarship About Women and Education, AERA, Montreal, April, 1983.

797.   ———. "Excellence and Curriculum: Alienation or Integration?" Paper read at the Symposium on Excellence and the Curriculum in honor of Mauritz Johnson, Albany, NY, November, 1983.

798.   ———. "Bringing Women Into Educational Thought." *Educational Theory 34* (1984): 341-353.

799.   ———. *Reclaiming a Conversation: The Ideal of the Educated Woman.* New Haven: Yale University Press, 1985.

800.   ———. "Becoming Educated: A Journey of Alienation or Integration?" Address to Division B, AERA, New Orleans, April, 1984.

801.   ———. "Redefining the Educated Person: Rethinking the Significance of Gender." *Educational Researcher 15* (1986): 6-10.

802.   Noddings, Nel. *Caring: A Feminist Approach to Ethics and Moral Education.* Berkeley and Los Angeles: University of California Press, 1984.

803.   Pagels, Elaine. *Adam, Eve, and the Serpent.* New York: Random House, 1988.

804.   Prather, Jane. "Why Can't Women Be More Like Men?" In Elizabeth S. Maccia et al., eds., *Women and Education,* pp. 50-59. Springfield, IL: Thomas, 1975.

805.   Rich, Adrienne. "Toward a Woman-Centered University." In *On Lies, Secrets and Silence,* pp. 125-155. New York: W. W. Norton, 1979.

806.   ———. "Conditions for Work: The Common World of Women." In *On Lies, Secrets and Silence,* pp. 203-214. New York: W. W. Norton, 1979.

807.   ———. "Taking Women Students Seriously." In *On Lies, Secrets and Silence,* pp. 237-245. New York: W. W. Norton, 1979.

808.   ———. "Claiming an Education." In *On Lies, Secrets and Silence*, pp. 231-235. New York: W. W. Norton, 1979.

CHAPTER 8

New Directions in Education: Gender as a Focus of Inquiry

why people be mad at me sometimes

> *they asked me to remember*
> *but they want me to remember*
> *their memories*
> *and i keep on remembering*
> *mine.*
> —*Lucille Clifton*

In the past three hundred and fifty years, issues in women's education have been transformed in many ways from an emphasis on exclusion to an emphasis on inclusion. More recently, issues in women's education have become increasingly intertwined with issues of difference not just of sex or gender, but of culture, class, religion, sexual orientation, ethnicity, and health. More important, perhaps, students of women's education have learned that gender is a construct that not only affects women, but men as well. Indeed, gender as a lens through which to study the complexities of social learning for males and females who participate in a wide variety of social groups is an important focus for further study.

It is a central theme of this section that knowledge gained in the study of women's education can be valuable as we find ourselves in the midst of an increasingly diverse society and as members of a global economy. The bibliography in this section, therefore, while it focuses on some of the same subjects as that in Chapter 7, is designed to acquaint the reader with new directions in education that incorporate, or can incorporate, gender as a focus of inquiry that will assist us in broadening our understanding of difference more generally.

Gender and Human Diversity

Perhaps the most significant fact of the latter part of the 20th century for citizens of the United States is that we are becoming more diverse in a number of fundamental ways. Indeed, a good deal of discussion is currently underway concerning the possibility that we will become so fragmented that we will not endure as a cohesive society. At the same time, it is likely that our diversity, if perceived as a resource and not a threat, may become our strongest feature. Certainly, we have for two centuries prided ourselves at least on the *idea* of pluralism, if not on the actual fact.

Central to the issue of whether and how we may learn to accommodate and appreciate the diversity we have is the question of how we will educate the next generations. While this has always been a problem for the United States, it appears that we are once again in a period when it is of critical and not just academic concern. For most of our history, the normative approach was to attempt to assimilate the children of difference through public schooling. To some extent, this process was reasonably successful, at least insofar as it did not result in insurrection. The process of assimilation, however, not only left many people out of the picture; it also was a very great waste of human cultural resources.

Scholars whose work appears in this section of the bibliography all, in one way or another, are calling for a more sophisticated understanding of social learning and its consequences. Whether the field is history or sociology or literature, they seek to free the disciplines from a unitary white middle-class focus, and acknowledge in research what is known in real life: that women's experience is multiple, that it originates in a wide variety of circumstances, and that commonalities and differences do not necessarily break down according to race and class lines (820).

What seems apparent is that scholarship on women has produced several conceptual and methodological resources that should be helpful in the study of other forms of difference. First, the study of women has produced the concept of *Other*, that is, a concept of what it means to be excluded from normative thought as well as day-to-day activities (819). From this concept comes a certain empathy, in theory if not always in practice, with oppression of all kinds directed toward all groups of people. It can be argued that without such a concept, it would be difficult to understand the overt and subtle ways in which certain individuals can be excluded from participation in and contribution to social life.

Second, those who have come to understand the influence of gender on the education of women have also described the parameters of that education in terms of education that is not schooling. This is significant when one is dealing with other populations whose education has been historically characterized by the most advanced forms of formal education. Closely related to this are the methodological approaches to the study of women's experience that emphasize the study of personal documents and biography that are often the only way of learning about the lives of people whose activities have not been part of the "public" domain.

Third, models of women's education that emphasize a concern with relationships may lead to a better understanding both of how similarities and differences in social learning are related to one another and to the larger educational enterprise. This, in turn, can extend the work on pedagogy that has emerged from a study of gender, and, presumably, assist us in developing more effective approaches to teaching and learning.

The belief that something *can* happen, of course, is no guarantee that it *will* happen. Clearly, the study of the education of women itself is not a major research agenda in many disciplines and there is much yet to do in the area. Moreover, although new forms of curriculum development and pedagogical methods have emerged from the study of gender and education, not everyone is willing to subscribe to them wholeheartedly. Therefore, the reader will also find in this section of the bibliography the many forms of resistance to such an agenda found among both policy makers, faculties, and students. Nevertheless, a considerable amount of work has already been done that has the potential to clarify and extend work on diversity.

Gender and Curriculum: The Problem of "Truth"

The difficulty of altering or transforming knowledge that is perceived as *truth* is probably incalculable. A number of scholars, however, have discussed the nature of these difficulties, as well as provided guidelines for transforming specific curricula.

Of particular interest is the work of Peggy McIntosh (874) and Mary Kay Thompson Tetreault (896) in synthesizing stages or phases through which curriculum transformation directed toward the inclusion of women's experience often moves. Briefly summarized (too briefly; the reader needs to explore the originals), five stages have been conceptualized. The first phase is the absence of the "Other," characterized by a belief that nothing is wrong, that knowledge exists apart from the knower but can and should be acquired because it is a "true" rendering of how the world really is. In the second phase, the "Other" is added, usually in terms of exceptional individuals like Queen Elizabeth or Jane Addams, who have participated in the public sphere and appear on the public record. McIntosh refers to this phase as a kind of "affirmative action program" for the disciplines (874). In the third phase, the "Other" is perceived as a problem. As more becomes known about the lives and work of women, their significance becomes a problem or an anomaly. In many ways, they do not exemplify a good "fit" with standard interpretations of knowledge and their "presence" in the field causes new questions to be raised about definitions of greatness and why these people have been excluded. The fourth phase of curriculum integration begins to focus on the "Other" as central to the knowledge base and the view that difference is not deficit begins to be acquired. Finally, in phase five, knowledge becomes transformed by a clear understanding of the difference that including the excluded makes. McIntosh notes that phase five thinking has hardly been conceived, let alone thoroughly developed (874). Nevertheless, it is a goal toward which many are working.

It is hard to underestimate the difficulty of attempting to transform knowledge, especially when the source of the transformation is the study of underrepresented and marginalized groups. Yet, many scholars in nearly all disciplines are currently working toward that end. The reader is advised, however, not to mistake enthusiasm for yet another set of "truths." Much remains to be done in the area of discovering not only new knowledge but also in understanding the complexities of its relation to knowledge that is currently available.

Gender and the "New" Pedagogy

Much of the work on gender and pedagogy derives from studies of differential treatment of boys and girls in classrooms, and from the experimental work of countless teachers at all levels of schooling in developing new methods of instruction that will more effectively help students learn. Not all of these methods have developed from a study of the education of women and girls. Indeed, some, such as inquiry teaching, have a history of their own that goes back at least to ancient Greece. However, many of the "new" instructional methods being discussed today in education have a good deal in common with what is usually thought of as "feminist pedagogy."

The impetus that led to the development of many of these methods was the acknowledgement that 1) girls and minority children of both genders were not having either the same educational experiences or the same educational outcomes as white, middle-class boys, and 2) that, in many cases, it was the interaction between teacher and student that accounted for a large percentage of difference in educational achievement and direction. The issue is a complicated one, of course. One problem is language, sometimes sexist, but often also unknowingly directed disproportionately toward boys rather than girls. Another is that traditional methods of teaching reward analytical behavior, toward which girls are not often socialized. A third problem is that differential expectations toward boys and girls are often communicated: the emphasis for boys is frequently that they will learn to deal with difficult situations and are expected to do a competent job; for girls, there is a tendency to emphasize deportment and neatness at the expense of academic quality. A fourth problem perceived by some scholars is that independent work and individual rewards, which are hallmarks of schooling, are sometimes at odds with the more relational, cooperative inclination of girls.

Consideration of these and other aspects of teaching has resulted in an approach to pedagogy that stresses cooperation and collaboration, the inclusion of life experiences as an avenue into subject matter, and a systematic attention to different "voices" (including those that derive from differences in gender socialization) as a way of deepening understanding of complex issues and events. Classroom instruction that emphasizes these elements also attempts to lower or do away with traditional discipline boundaries, in the reasonable belief that in history or any other subject under study, these boundaries are artificial and do not reflect the experience of real people.

Items in the bibliography for this section again represent only a selection of the work on gender and pedagogy. Indeed, it would probably be possible to do an entire bibliographical work on just this subject as it has been developed in the past ten years. However, this will serve to introduce the reader to the area and, perhaps, stimulate further interest.

Gender and the Preparation of Professional Educators

In this final section of the bibliography are listed a variety of works on the effort to alter the preparation of professional educators. It is surprising that more attention has not been given to the preparation of teachers and administrators in schools, given the influence they have on the education of all children.

Several issues are paramount in this literature. First, and perhaps most frequent, are works on the access of women to positions of authority in public, coeducational schools. A second area of interest is the nature of teaching as a profession in terms of women's life cycles. Biklin, for example, has found that many women teachers, who often move in and out of the profession to have children or otherwise care for family members, still think of themselves as teachers even when they are not working in that capacity (935). This is at considerable variance with the self-concept of many women who are, for one reason or another, at home. In general terms, they do not often think of themselves as members of their profession or job category unless they are, in fact, working at it.

A third focus of this section of the bibliography is the bias of teacher education texts and the traditional modeling of the teaching act that many preservice teachers observe. Included in this area is considerable attention to the fact that women are more than underrepresented in educational theory, and that a variety of ways of knowing are not exemplified in methodological literature for teachers.

A fourth area of interest among those who are concerned with the preparation of education professionals is the influence of race and class as it interacts with gender in teaching and learning. This is an area too little studied to this point but one that reflects the growing national preoccupation with diversity. As was mentioned earlier in this chapter, it is here that an understanding of gender as it has been developed through the study of women's educational and social experience can serve as a foundation for the more complex work that needs to be done.

Clearly, the work exemplified in Part III of this volume is work that is unfinished—some would say, barely begun. At this stage of its development, it is hardly possible to begin to describe it for we currently lack sufficient language to talk about the degree of complexity to which it refers. It is thus also not possible at this stage to begin to synthesize the work that women (and some men) are doing to alter the educational experiences of girls and boys. Perhaps, after a century or so, it will be possible to put these efforts into the kind of perspective that we are able to do for the work of women of the 19th century. For the present, however, we can hope that works like this volume will help to stimulate the interest required to continue the study of the education of women.

BIBLIOGRAPHY

Gender and Human Diversity

809.   Andersen, Margaret L. "Women's Studies/Black Studies: Learning from Our Common Pasts/Forging a Common Future." In Marilyn R. Schuster and Susan R. Van Dyne, eds., *Women's Place in the Academy*, pp. 62-72. Totowa, NJ: Rowman and Allenheld, 1985.

810.   Aptheker, Bettina, ed. *Women's Legacy: Essays on Race, Sex and Class in American History*. Amherst: University of Massachusetts Press, 1982.

811.   Arnot, Madeleine. *Race and Gender*. New York: Pergamon
        Press, 1985.

812.   Banks, J. and Banks, C., eds. *Multicultural Education: Issues
        and Perspectives*. Boston: Allyn and Bacon, 1989.

813.   Borman, Kathryn M., Mueninghoff, Elaine, and Piazza,
        Shirley. "Urban Appalachian Girls and Young Women:
        Bowing to No One." In Lois Weis, ed., *Class, Race, and
        Gender in American Education*, pp. 230-248. Albany, NY:
        State University of New York Press, 1988.

814.   Butler, Johnella E. "Transforming the Curriculum: Teaching
        About Women of Color." In J. Banks and C. Banks, eds.,
        Multicultural Education: Issues and Perspectives, pp.
        145-163. Boston: Allyn and Bacon, 1989.

815.   ———. "Complicating the Question: Black Studies and
        Women's Studies." In Marilyn R. Schuster and Susan R.
        Van Dyne, eds., *Women's Place in the Academy*, pp.
        73-86. Totowa, NJ: Rowman and Allenheld, 1985.

816.   ——— and Schmitz, Betty. "Different Voices: A Model Institute
        for Integrating Women of Color Into Undergraduate
        American Literature and History Courses." *Radical
        Teacher 37* (1990): 4-9.

817.   *Common Differences Between Black and White Women—
        Changing the Way We Think About and Teach Women's
        Experiences and the Humanities*. Durham, NC: Center for
        Research on Women, Duke University, 1984.

818.   Davis, Angela. *Women, Race and Class*. New York: Random
        House, 1981.

819.   deBeauvoir, Simone. *The Second Sex* (1949). Trans. by H. M.
        Parshley. New York: Bantam, 1961.

820.   DuBois, Ellen C. and Ruiz, V. L., eds. *Unequal Sisters: A
        Multicultural History of Women in the U.S.* New York:
        Routledge, 1990.

821.   Franklin, Vincent P. and Anderson, James D., eds. *New Perspectives on Black Educational History*. Boston: G. K. Hall, 1978.

822.   Giddings, Paula. *When and Where I Enter: The Impact of Black Women in Race and Sex in America*. New York: William Morrow and Co., 1984.

823.   Grant, Carl A. and Sleeter, Christine E. "Race, Class, Gender, Exceptionality, and Educational Reform." In J. Banks and C. Banks, eds., *Multicultural Education: Issues and Perspectives*, pp. 46-65. Boston: Allyn and Bacon, 1989.

824.   hooks, bell. *Ain't I a Woman? Black Women and Feminism*. Boston: South End Press, 1981.

825.   Humphries, Sheila, ed. *Women and Minorities in Science: Strategies for Increasing Participation*. Boulder, CO: American Association for the Advancement of Science, 1982.

826.   Jacobowitz, Tina. "Relation of Sex, Achievement, and Scientific Self-Concept to the Science Career Preferences of Black Students." *Journal of Research in Science Teaching 20* (1983): 621-628.

827.   Janiewski, Dolores. *Sisterhood Denied: Race, Gender, and Class in a New South Community*. Philadelphia: Temple University Press, 1985.

828.   Lamonte, Ruth B. "Minority Women and American Schooling." *Educational Horizons 60* (1981): 16-21.

829.   La Rodgers-Rose, Frances, ed. *The Black Woman*. Beverly Hills, CA: Sage, 1980.

830.   Lerner, Gerda. *Black Women in White America: A Documentary History*. New York: Pantheon, 1972.

831.   ———. "Black and White Women in Interaction and Confrontation." In *The Majority Finds Its Past*, pp. 94-111. New York: Oxford University Press, 1979.

832. Lightfoot, Sara Lawrence. "Family-School Interactions: The Cultural Image of Mothers and Teachers." *Signs: Journal of Women in Culture and Society 3* (1977): 395-408.

833. ———. "Socialization and Education of Young Black Girls in School." In Sari Knopp Biklen and Marilyn B. Brannigan, eds., *Women and Educational Leadership*, pp. 139-164. Lexington, MA: Heath, 1980.

834. McCarthy, Cameron and Apple, Michael W. "Race, Class, and Gender in American Educational Research: Toward a Nonsynchronous Parallelist Position." In Lois Weis, ed., *Class, Race, and Gender in American Education*, pp. 9-39. Albany, NY: State University of New York Press, 1988.

835. McKay, Nellie. "Black Woman Professor--White University." In Renate D. Klein and Deborah Lynn Steinberg, eds., *Radical Voices: A Decade of Feminist Resistance*, pp. 36-41. New York: Pergamon Press, 1989.

836. Mercer, Jane R. "Alternative Paradigms for Assessment in a Pluralistic Society." In J. Banks and C. Banks, eds., *Multicultural Education: Issues and Perspectives*, pp. 285-304. Boston: Allyn and Bacon, 1989.

837. Ogbu, John U. "Class Stratification, Racial Stratification, and Schooling." In Lois Weis, ed., *Class, Race, and Gender in American Education*, pp. 163-182. Albany, NY: State University of New York Press, 1988.

838. Ortiz, Flora Ida. *Career Patterns in Education: Women, Men and Minorities*. South Hadley, MA: Bergin and Garvey, 1988.

839. ———. "Hispanic-American Children's Experiences in Classrooms: A Comparison between Hispanic and Non-Hispanic Children." In Lois Weis, ed., *Class, Race, and Gender in American Education*, pp. 63-86. Albany, NY: State University of New York Press, 1988.

840. Rosenfelt, Deborah S. "Integrating Cross-Cultural Perspectives in the Curriculum: Working for Change in

the California State Universities." *Radical Teacher 37* (1990): 10-13.

841.   Scott-Jones, Diane and Clark, Maxine L. "The School Experiences of Black Girls: The Interaction of Gender, Race, and Socioeconomic Status." *Phi Delta Kappan 67* (1986): 520-526.

842.   Sells, Lucy. "The Mathematics Filter and the Education of Women and Minorities." In L. H. Fox, L. Brody, and D. Tobin, eds., *Women and the Mathematical Mystique.* Baltimore: Johns Hopkins University Press, 1976.

843.   Simms, Richard L. and Contreras, Gloria, eds. *Racism and Sexism: Responding to the Challenge.* Washington, DC: National Council of Social Studies, 1980.

844.   Sleeter, Christine E. and Grant, Carl A. "A Rationale for Integrating Race, Gender, and Social Class." In Lois Weis, ed., *Class, Race, and Gender in American Education,* pp. 144-160. Albany: State University of New York Press, 1988.

845.   Smith, Barbara, ed. *Home Girls: A Black Feminist Anthology.* New York: Kitchen Table: Women of Color Press, 1983.

846.   Solomon, R. Patrick. "Black Cultural Forms in Schools: A Cross National Comparison." In Lois Weis, ed., *Class, Race, and Gender in American Education,* pp. 249-265. Albany: State University of New York Press, 1988.

847.   Stanlaw, James and Peshkin, Alan. "Black Visibility in a Multi-Ethnic High School." In Lois Weis, ed., *Class, Race and Gender in American Education,* pp. 209-229. Albany, NY: State University of New York Press, 1988.

848.   Steady, Filomena C., ed. *The Black Woman Cross-Culturally.* Cambridge: Schenkman Publishing Co., 1981.

849.   Stoner, K. Lynn, ed. *Latinas of the Americas: A Source Book.* New York: Garland, 1989.

850.   Van Horne, Winston A., ed. *Ethnicity and Women.* Madison: University of Wisconsin System American Ethnic Studies

Coordinating Committee/Urban Corridor Consortium, 1986.

851.   Velez, William. "Why Hispanic Students Fail: Factors Affecting Attrition in High Schools." In Jeanne H. Ballentine, ed., *Schools and Society: A Unified Reader, 2nd ed.*, pp. 380-388. Mountain View, CA: Mayfield, 1989.

852.   Walker, S. and Barton, L., eds. *Gender, Class and Education.* Sussex: Falmer Press, 1983.

853.   Weis, Lois, ed. *Class, Race, and Gender in American Education.* Albany, NY: State University of New York Press, 1988.

854.   ———. "Introduction." In Lois Weis, ed., *Class, Race and Gender in American Education*, pp. 1-7. Albany, NY: State University of New York Press, 1988.

Gender and the Curriculum: The Problem of "Truth"

855.   Aiken, Susan et al. "Trying Transformations: Curriculum Integration and the Problem of Resistance." In E. Minnich, J. O'Barr, and R. Rosenfeld, eds., *Reconstructing the Academy*, pp. 104-124. Chicago: University of Chicago Press, 1988.

856.   Andersen, Margaret L. "Changing the Curriculum in Higher Education." In E. Minnich, J. O'Barr, and R. Rosenfeld, eds., *Reconstructing the Academy*, pp. 36-68. Chicago: University of Chicago Press, 1988.

857.   Boneparth, Ellen. "Integrating Materials on Women: American Government." *News for Teachers of Political Science 26* (1980): 1-7.

858.   Brody, Celeste M. "Do Instructional Materials Reinforce Sex Stereotyping?" *Educational Leadership 31* (1973): 119-122.

859.   Bunch, Charlotte and Pollack, Sandra, eds. *Learning Our Way: Essays in Feminist Education.* Trumansburg, NY: Crossing Press, 1983.

860.   Degler, Carl. "What the Women's Movement Has Done to American History." In Elizabeth Langland and Walter Gove, eds., *A Feminist Perspective in the Academy*, pp. 67-85. Chicago: University of Chicago Press, 1983.

861.   Dinnerstein, M., O'Donnell, M., and MacCorquodale, P. "How to Integrate Women's Studies into the Curriculum." Working Paper No. 9. Southwest Institute for Research on Women, 1982.

862.   —— and Schmitz, Betty, eds. *Ideas and Resources for Integrating Women's Studies into the Curriculum, Vol. I and II.* Western States Project on Women and the Curriculum and the Southwest Institute for Research on Women, 1986.

863.   Federbush, Marsha. "The Sex Problem of School Math Books." In Judith Stacey et al., eds., *And Jill Came Tumbling After: Sexism in American Education.* New York: Dell, 1974.

864.   Feminists on Children's Media. "A Feminist Looks at Children's Books." In Elizabeth S. Maccia et al., eds., *Women and Education*, pp. 212-225. Springfield, IL: Thomas, 1975.

865.   Filene, Peter G. "Integrating Women's History and Regular History." *The History Teacher 8* (1980): 483-492.

866.   Fowlkes, Diane L. and McClure, Charlotte S., eds. *Feminist Visions: Toward a Transformation of the Liberal Arts Curriculum.* University, AL: The University of Alabama Press, 1984.

867.   Frasher, Ramona and Walker, Anabelle. "Sex Roles in Early Reading Textbooks." In Elizabeth S. Maccia et al., eds., *Women and Education*, pp. 226-238. Springfield, IL: Thomas, 1975.

868.   Froschl, Merle and Sprung, Barbara. *Resources for Educational Equity: A Guide for Grades Pre-Kindergarten-12.* New York: Garland, 1988.

869. Howe, Florence. "Feminist Scholarship: The Extent of the Revolution." *Change 14* (1982): 12-20.

870. Hulme, Marylin A. "Mirror, Mirror on the Wall: Biased Reflections in Textbooks and Instructional Materials." In Anne O'Brien Carelli, ed., *Sex Equity in Education: Readings and Strategies*, pp. 187-208. Springfield, IL: Thomas, 1988.

871. Keller, Evelyn Fox. *Reflections on Gender and Science*. New Haven: Yale University Press, 1985.

872. Marland, Michael. "Curriculum Matters." In Michael Marland, ed., *Sex Differentiation and Schooling*, pp. 143-162. London: Heinemann Educational Books, 1983.

873. McIntosh, Peggy. "The Study of Women: Implications for Reconstructing the Liberal Arts Disciplines." *The Forum For Liberal Education 4* (1981).

874. ———. "Interactive Phases of Curricular Re-Vision: A Feminist Perspective." Working Paper No. 124, Wellesley College Center for Research on Women, 1983.

875. McLure, Gail T. "Eliminate Sex Bias in the Curriculum." *Educational Leadership 31* (1973): 111-113.

876. Nilsen, Aleen Pace. "Women in Children's Literature." In Elizabeth S. Maccia et al., eds., *Women and Education*, pp. 198-211. Springfield, IL: Thomas, 1975.

877. O'Donnell, Richard W. "Sex Bias in Primary Social Studies Textbooks." *Educational Leadership 31* (1973): 137-141.

878. Pinar, William F. and Miller, Janet L. "Feminist Curriculum Theory: Notes on the American Field, 1982." *Journal of Educational Thought 16* (1982): 217-224.

879. Rosenberg, Max. "Evaluate Your Textbooks for Racism, Sexism!" *Educational Leadership 31* (1973): 107-109.

880. Rosovsky, Candace. "A Trickle or a Flood? Women and Curricular Choice in University English Departments." *Radical Teacher 37* (1990): 34-38.

881. Rosser, Sue V. "Integrating the Feminist Perspective into Courses in Introductory Biology." In Marilyn R. Schuster and Susan R. Van Dyne, eds., *Women's Place in the Academy*, pp. 258-276. Totowa, NJ: Rowman and Allenheld, 1985.

882. ———. *Female Friendly Science: Applying Women's Studies Methods and Theories to Attract Students*. New York: Pergamon Press, 1990.

883. Salem, Greta and Sharkey, Stephen. "Transforming the Social Sciences." In Marilyn R. Schuster and Susan R. Van Dyne, eds., *Women's Place in the Academy*, pp. 232-257. Totowa, NJ: Rowman and Allenheld, 1985.

884. Schilb, John. "Transforming a Course in American Literary Realism." In Marilyn R. Schuster and Susan R. Van Dyne, eds., *Women's Place in the Academy*, pp. 201-220. Totowa, NJ: Rowman and Allenheld, 1985.

885. Schmitz, B; Dinnerstein, M.; and Mairs, N. "Initiating a Curriculum Integration Project: Lessons from the Campus and the Region." In Marilyn R. Schuster and Susan R. Van Dyne, eds., *Women's Place in the Academy*, pp. 116-129. Totowa, NJ: Rowman and Allenheld, 1985.

886. ———, ed. *Integrating Women's Studies into the Curriculum: A Guide and Bibliography*. Old Westbury, NY: The Feminist Press, 1985.

887. Schuster, Marilyn R. and Van Dyne, Susan R., eds. *Women's Place in the Academy*. Totowa, NJ: Rowman and Allenheld, 1985.

888. ———. "Curricular Change for the Twenty-First Century: Why Women?" In Marilyn R. Schuster and Susan R. Van Dyne, eds., *Women's Place in the Academy*, pp. 3-12. Totowa, NJ: Rowman and Allenheld, 1985.

889. ———. "Stages of Curriculum Transformation." In Marilyn R. Schuster and Susan R. Van Dyne, eds., *Women's Place in the Academy*, pp. 13-29. Totowa, NJ: Rowman and Allenheld, 1985.

890. ———. "Changing the Institution." In Marilyn R. Schuster and Susan R. Van Dyne, eds., *Women's Place in the Academy*, pp. 89-97. Totowa, NJ: Rowman and Allenheld, 1985.

891. ———. "The Changing Classroom." In Marilyn R. Schuster and Susan R. Van Dyne, eds., *Women's Place in the Academy*, pp. 161-171. Totowa, NJ: Rowman and Allenheld, 1985.

892. Spanier, Bonnie, Bloom, Alexander, and Boroviak, D., eds., *Toward a Balanced Curriculum: A Sourcebook for Initiating Gender Integration Projects*. Cambridge: Schenkman, 1984.

893. Stefflre, Buford. "Run, Mama, Run: Women Workers in Elementary Readers." In Elizabeth S. Maccia et al., eds., *Women and Education*, pp. 239-244. Springfield, IL: Thomas, 1975.

894. Stimpson, Catherine. "The New Scholarship About Women: The State of the Art." *Annals of Scholarship 2* (1980): 2-14.

895. Sutherland, Margaret B. "Anxiety, Aspirations and the Curriculum." In Michael Marland, ed., *Sex Differentiation and Schooling*, pp. 60-71. London: Heinemann Educational Books, 1983.

896. Tetreault, Mary Kay Thompson. "Rethinking Women, Gender, and the Social Studies." *Social Education 51* (1987): 170-178.

897. Trecker, Janice Law. "Women in U.S. History High School Textbooks." In Elizabeth S. Maccia et al., eds., *Women and Education*, pp. 252-271. Springfield, IL: Thomas, 1975.

898. ———. "Woman's Place is in the Curriculum." In Elizabeth S. Maccia et al., ed., *Women and Education*, pp. 272-281. Springfield, IL: Thomas, 1975.

899. Warren, Joyce W. "Gender and Literature: Teaching 'The (Other) American Tradition.'" *Radical Teacher 37* (1990): 30-33.

900.   Women on Words and Images. *Help Wanted: Sexism in Career
        Education Materials*. Princeton, NJ: Women on Words
        and Images, 1975.

Gender and the "New" Pedagogy

901.   Becker, J. R. "Differential Treatment of Females and Males in
        Mathematics Classes." *Journal for Research in
        Mathematics Education 12* (1981): 40-53.

902.   Brophy, J. E. and Good, T. L. "Teachers' Communication of
        Differential Expectations for Children's Classroom
        Performance: Some Behavioral Data." *Journal of
        Educational Psychology 61* (1970): 365-374.

903.   Campbell, Patricia B. "General Educational Practices for
        Promoting Sex Equity." In Susan S. Klein, ed.,
        Handbook for Achieving Sex Equity through Education,
        pp. 163-165. Baltimore: Johns Hopkins University Press,
        1985.

904.   ———. "What's a Nice Girl Like You Doing in Math Class?"
        Phi Delta Kappan 67 (1986): 516-520.

905.   Culley, Margo and Portugues, Catherine, eds. *Gendered
        Subjects: The Dynamics of Feminist Teaching*. Boston:
        Routledge and Kegan Paul, 1985.

906.   Flood, Craig. "Stereotyping and Classroom Interactions." In
        Anne O'Brien Carelli, ed., *Sex Equity in Education:
        Readings and Strategies*, pp. 109-125. Springfield, IL:
        Thomas, 1988.

907.   Grant, Linda. "Race-Gender Status, Classroom Interaction,
        and Children's Socialization in Elementary School." In L.
        Wilkinson and C. Marrett, eds., *Gender Influences in
        Classroom Interaction*, pp. 57-77. New York: Academic
        Press, 1985.

908.   Harvey, Glen. "Finding Reality Among the Myths: Why What
        You Thought About Sex Equity Isn't So." *Phi Delta
        Kappan 67* (1986): 509-512.

909.   Howe, Florence. "Sexual Stereotypes Start Early." In
        Elizabeth S. Maccia et al., eds., *Women and Education*,
        pp. 8-21. Springfield, IL: Thomas, 1975.

910.   Jones, M. Gail. "Gender Bias in Classroom Interaction."
        Contemporary Education 60 (1989): 218-222.

911.   Leinhardt, Gaea, Seewald, Andrea, and Engel, Mary.
        "Learning What's Taught: Sex Differences in
        Interaction." *Journal of Educational Psychology 71*
        (1979): 432-439.

912.   Levy, Betty and Judith Stacey. "Sexism in Elementary
        School: A Backward and Forward Look." *Phi Delta
        Kappan 55* (1973): 105-109, 123.

913.   Lockheed, Marlaine E. "Sex Equity in Classroom
        Organization and Climate." In Susan S. Klein, ed.,
        Handbook for Achieving Sex Equity through Education.
        Baltimore: Johns Hopkins University Press, 1985.

914.   Maher, Frances. "Classroom Pedagogy and the New
        Scholarship on Women." In Margo Culley and Catherine
        Portuges, eds., *Gendered Subjects: The Dynamics of
        Feminist Teaching.* London: Routledge and Kegan Paul,
        1985.

915.   ———. "Pedagogies for the Gender-Balanced Classroom."
        Journal of Thought 20 (1985): 48-64.

916.   ———. "Inquiry Teaching and Feminist Pedagogy." *Social
        Education 51* (1987): 186-192.

917.   ———. "Toward a Richer Theory of Feminist Pedagogy: A
        Comparison of Liberation and Gender Models for
        Teaching and Learning." *Journal of Education 169*
        (1987): 91-100.

918.   Marland, Michael. "Guidance and Pastoral Care." In Michael
        Marland, ed., *Sex Differentiation and Schooling*, pp.
        117-122. London: Heinemann Educational Books, 1983.

919.   ———. "Should the Sexes be Separated?" In Michael Marland,
         ed., *Sex Differentiation and Schooling*, pp. 181-186.
         London: Heinemann Educational Books, 1983.

920.   Sadker, Myra. "Sexism in Schools." *Journal of Teacher
         Education 26* (1975): 317-322.

921.   ———, David Sadker and Lynette Long. "Gender and
         Educational Equality." In J. Banks and C. Banks, eds.,
         Multicultural Education: Issues and Perspectives, pp.
         106-122. Boston: Allyn and Bacon, 1989.

922.   ——— and Sadker, David. "Sexism in the Classroom: From
         Grade School to Graduate School." *Phi Delta Kappan 67*
         (1986): 512-515.

923.   Sears, Pauline and David Feldman. "Teacher Interaction with
         Boys and Girls." *The National Elementary Principal 46*
         (1966): 30-35.

924.   Shakeshaft, Charol. "A Gender at Risk." *Phi Delta Kappan 67*
         (1986): 499-503.

925.   Sklar, Kathryn Kish. "A Conceptual Framework for the
         Teaching of U. S. Women's History." *The History Teacher
         13* (1980): 471-481.

926.   Spatig, Linda. "Learning to Manage the Heart: Gender
         Relations in an Elementary Classroom." *Educational
         Foundations 2* (1988): 27-44.

927.   Spender, Dale. " 'Telling How It Is': Language and Gender in
         the Classroom." In Michael Marland, ed., *Sex
         Differentiation and Schooling*, pp. 98-116. London:
         Heinemann Educational Books, 1983.

928.   Wilkinson, L. and Marrett, C., eds. *Gender Influences in
         Classroom Interaction*. New York: Academic Press, 1985.

Gender and the Preparation of Education Professionals

929.   Antonucci, Toni. "The Need for Female Role Models in
         Education." In Sari Knopp Biklen and Marilyn B.

Brannigan, eds., *Women and Educational Leadership*, pp. 185-195. Lexington, MA: Heath, 1980.

930. Bach, Louise. "Of Women, School Administration, and Discipline." *Phi Delta Kappan 57* (1976): 463-466.

931. Berrey, M. C., ed. *Women in Educational Administration.* Washington, DC: National Association of Women Deans, Administrators, and Counselors, 1979.

932. Biklen, Sari Knopp. "Introduction: Barriers to Equity— Women, Educational Leadership and Social Change." In Sari Knopp Biklen and Marilyn B. Brannigan, eds., *Women and Educational Leadership*, pp. 1-23. Lexington, MA: Heath, 1980.

933. —— and Brannigan, Marilyn B., eds. *Women and Educational Leadership.* Lexington, MA: Heath, 1980.

934. —— and Shakeshaft, Charol. "The New Scholarship on Women." In Susan S. Klein, ed., *Handbook for Achieving Sex Equity through Education*, pp. 44-52. Baltimore: Johns Hopkins University Press, 1985.

935. ——. "'I Have Always Worked': Elementary Schoolteaching as a Career." *Phi Delta Kappan 67* (1986): 504-508.

936. Burstyn, Joan. "Historical Perspectives on Women in Educational Leadership." In Sari Knopp Biklen and Marilyn B. Brannigan, eds., *Women and Educational Leadership*, pp. 65-75. Lexington, MA: Heath, 1980.

937. ——. "Integrating the New Scholarship on Women into Required Courses in Schools of Education." *Educational Researcher 15* (1986): 11-13.

938. Clement, Jacqueline. "Sex Bias in School Administration." In Sari Knopp Biklen and Marilyn B. Brannigan, eds., *Women and Educational Leadership*, pp. 131-137. Lexington, MA: Heath, 1980.

939. Coffin, G. C. and Ekstrom, Ruth B. "Roadblocks to Women's Careers in Educational Administration." In M. C. Berrey, ed., *Women in Educational Administration*, pp. 53-63.

Washington, DC: National Association of Women Deans, Administrators and Counselors, 1979.

940.   Cushner, Kenneth, McClelland, Averil, and Safford, Philip. *Human Diversity in Education: An Integrative Approach.* New York: McGraw-Hill, 1992.

941.   Dale, Charlene T. "Women Are Still Missing Persons in Administrative and Supervisory Jobs." *Educational Leadership 31* (1973): 123-127.

942.   Doughty, Rosie. "The Black Female Administrator: Woman in a Double Bind." In Sari Knopp Biklen and Marilyn B. Brannigan, eds., *Women and Educational Leadership*, pp. 165-174. Lexington, MA: Heath, 1980.

943.   Erickson, H. Lynn. "Conflict and the Female Principal." *Phi Delta Kappan 67* (1985): 288-291.

944.   Fauth, Gloria C. "Women in Educational Administration: A Research Profile." *The Educational Forum 49* (1984): 65-79.

945.   Feldman, Jean R., Jorgensen, Margaret, and Poling, Eve. "Illusions: Women in Educational Administration." In Anne O'Brien Carelli, ed., *Sex Equity in Education: Readings and Strategies*, pp. 333-353. Springfield, IL: Thomas, 1988.

946.   Fishel, Andrew and Pottker, Janice. "Women in Educational Governance: A Statistical Portrait." *Educational Researcher 3* (1974): 4-7.

947.   Fishel, Andrew and Pottker, Janice. "Performance of Women Principals: A Review of Behavior and Attitudinal Studies." In Janice Pottker and Andrew Fishel, eds., *Sex Bias in the Schools*. Cranbury, NJ: Associated University Presses, 1977.

948.   Ginzburg, Mark B. "Teacher Education and Class and Gender Relations: A Critical Analysis of Historical Studies of Teacher Education." *Educational Foundations 1* (1987): 4-36.

949.   Gribskov, Margaret. "Feminism and the Woman School
        Administrator." In Sari Knopp Biklen and Marilyn B.
        Brannigan, eds., *Women and Educational Leadership*, pp.
        77-91. Lexington, MA: Heath, 1980.

950.   Kane, Roslyn. *Sex Discrimination in Education: A Study of
        Employment Practices Affecting Professional Personnel.*
        Washington, DC: National Center for Educational
        Statistics, April, 1976.

951.   Kmetz, John T. and Willower, Donald J. "Elementary School
        Principals' Work Behavior." *Educational Administration
        Quarterly 18* (1982): 62-78.

952.   Laird, Susan. "Reforming 'Woman's True Profession': A Case
        for 'Feminist Pedagogy' in Teacher Education?" *Harvard
        Educational Review 58* (1988): 449-463.

953.   Lather, Patti. "Reeducating Educators: Sex Equity in Teacher
        Education." *Educational Horizons 60* (1981): 36-40.

954.   ———. "Research as Praxis." *Harvard Educational Review 56*
        (1986): 257-273.

955.   ———. "Feminist Perspectives on Empowering Research
        Methodologies." Paper prepared for the 8th Annual
        Curriculum Theorizing Conference, Bergamo Center,
        Dayton, Ohio, October 22-25, 1986.

956.   Leach, Mary. "Teacher Education and Reform: 'What's Sex
        Got to Do with It?'" *Educational Foundations 2* (1988):
        4-14.

957.   Leck, Glorianne M. "Examining Gender as a Foundation
        Within the Foundational Studies of Education." *Teachers
        College Record* (Spring 1990).

958.   Maienza, Janice Grow. "The Superintendency: Characteristics
        of Access for Men and Women." *Educational
        Administration Quarterly 22* (1986): 59-79.

959.   McCall, Ava L. "Care and Nurturance in Teaching: A Case
        Study." *Journal of Teacher Education 40* (1989): 39-44.

960.   McClelland, Averil E. "Gender and the Social Foundations: A
         Call to Action." *Educational Foundations 2* (1988): 15-26.

961.   McClure, John and McClure, Gail. "The Case of the
         Vanishing Woman: Implications for the Preparation of
         Women Educational Administrators." *UCEA Review*
         (1974): 609.

962.   McCune, Shirley and Matthews, Martha. "Eliminating
         Sexism: Teacher Education and Change." *Journal of
         Teacher Education 26* (1975): 294-300.

963.   Meskin, Joan. "The Performance of Women School
         Administrators: A Review of the Literature."
         Administrators Notebook 19 (1974).

964.   Mitrano, Barbara S. "Feminism and Curriculum Theory:
         Implications for Teacher Education." *Journal of
         Curriculum Theory 3* (1981): 5-85.

965.   Noddings, Nel. "Fidelity in Teaching, Teacher Education, and
         Research for Teaching." *Harvard Educational Review 56*
         (1986): 496-511.

966.   Picker, Ann M. "Female Educational Administrators: Coping
         in a Basically Male Environment." *Educational Horizons
         58* (1980): 145-149.

967.   Reinharz, Shulamit. "The Career Controversy for Women."
         Educational Horizons 64 (1986): 136-139.

968.   Reitman, Sanford W. "Institutional Sexism, the Contemporary
         Teaching Crisis, and Teacher Education." *Journal of
         Teacher Education 26* (1975): 293.

969.   Sadker, Myra P. and Sadker, David M. "Sexism in
         Teacher-Education Texts." *Harvard Educational Review
         50* (1980): 36-46.

970.   —— and Hicks, Tom. "The One-Percent Solution? Sexism in
         Teacher Education Texts." *Phi Delta Kappan* 61 (1980):
         550-553.

971.   ———. "Sex Equity in Teacher Preparation: A Priority for the Eighties." *Journal of Teacher Education 31* (1980): 4-5.

972.   ———. *Beyond Pictures and Pronouns: Sexism in Teacher Education Textbooks*. Washington, DC: U. S. Government Printing Office, 1981.

973.   Sadker, David and Sadker, Myra. "The Treatment of Sex Equity in Teacher Education." In Susan S. Klein, ed., *Handbook for Achieving Sex Equity through Education*, pp. 145-161. Baltimore: Johns Hopkins University Press, 1985.

974.   Schmuck, Patricia A. "Deterrents to Women's Careers in School Management." *Sex Roles 1* (1975): 9-353.

975.   ———. "Changing Women's Representation in School Management: A Systems Perspective." In Sari Knopp Biklen and Marilyn B. Brannigan, eds., *Women and Educational Leadership*, pp. 239-259. Lexington, MA: Heath, 1980.

976.   ———., Charters, W. W., Jr., and Carlson, R. O., eds. *Educational Policy and Management: Sex Differentials*. New York: Academic Press, 1981.

977.   Shakeshaft, Charol. "Strategies for Overcoming the Barriers to Women in Educational Administration." In Susan S. Klein, ed., *Handbook for Achieving Sex Equity through Education*, pp. 124-144. Baltimore: Johns Hopkins University Press, 1985.

978.   Strober, Myra H. and Tyack, David. "Sexual Asymmetry in Educational Employment: Male Managers and Female Teachers." Draft Report, Institute for Research on Educational Finance and Governance, Stanford University, February, 1979.

979.   ———. "Why Do Women Teach and Men Manage? A Report on Research on Schools." *Signs: Journal of Women in Culture and Society 5* (1980): 494-503.

980.   Tetreault, Mary Kay Thompson. "The Journey from Male-
        Defined to Gender-Balanced Education." *Theory Into
        Practice 25* (1986): 227-234.

981.   —— and Braunger, Jane. "Improving Mentor Teacher
        Seminars: Feminist Theory and Practice at Lewis and
        Clark College." In *Building Bridges for Educational
        Reform: New Approaches to Teacher Education*, pp. 63-83.
        Ames, IO: Iowa State University Press, 1989.

982.   Tyack, David B. and Strober, Myra H. "Jobs and Gender: A
        History of the Structuring of Educational Employment
        by Sex." In Patricia A. Schmuck, W. W. Charters, Jr.,
        and Richard O. Carlson, eds., *Educational Policy and
        Management: Sex Differentials*, pp. 131-52. New York:
        Academic Press, 1981.

983.   Tyack, David and Hansot, Elisabeth. *Managers of Virtue:
        Public School Leadership in America, 1820-1980*. New
        York: Basic Books, 1982.

984.   Weiler, Kathleen. *Women Teaching for Change: Gender, Class
        and Power*. South Hadley, MA: Bergin and Garvey, 1988.

INDEX A

AUTHORS
(Numbers in index indicate entry numbers.)

Abbott, Edith
299, 375
Abrahams, Harold J.
558
Abrams, Annie
054
Acker, Joan
444
Addison, Linda
740
Agre, Gene P.
718
Aiken, Susan
855
Alaya, Flavia
230
Alcott, Bronson
202
Alcott, Louisa May
231
Alic, Margaret
019
Allain, Violet Anselmini
719
Allmendinger, David, F., Jr.
544
Ames, Azel
300
Andersen, Margaret L.
809, 856
Anderson, James D.
376, 575, 821
Antler, Joyce
529, 530, 531, 591, 592
Antonucci, Toni
929

Apple, Michael
834
Aptheker, Bettina
810
Arch, Elizabeth
707
Armstrong, J. E.
576
Arnot, Madeleine
720, 721, 811
As, Berit
777
Ascham, Roger
111
Astin, Helen S.
593
Atkinson, Jane
707
Auwers, Linda
175, 176
Axtell, James
177

Bach, Louise
930
Bacon, Martha
232
Bailey, Ebenezer
203
Bailey, Nettie F.
499
Bailyn, Bernard
001
Bainton, Roland H.
093, 094, 095

Rosenberg, Charles
265
Rosenberg, Max
879
Rosenberg, Rosalind
569, 646, 675, 696
Rosenberry, Lois I.
521
Rosenfeld, Rachel
694
Rosenfelt, Deborah S.
840
Rosovsky, Candace
880
Rosser, Sue V.
881, 882
Rossi, Alice S.
570, 676, 677
Rossiter, Margaret W.
432, 433
Rota, Tiziana
557
Rothman, Sheila
678
Rousmaniere, J.
540
Rousseau, Jean Jacques
121
Rowbottom, Sheila
679
Ruddick, Sara
321
Rudolph, Fredrick
647
Ruether, Rosemary Radford
478
Ruiz, V. L.
820
Rury, John
017, 168, 590, 648
Rush, Benjamin
225

Russell, Rosalind
107
Russo, L. N.
749
Ryan, Mary P.
159, 263

Sachs, Hannelore
090
Sack, Saul
649
Sacks, Karen Brodkin
322
Sadker, David
762, 763, 764, 921, 922,
969-973
Sadker, Myra
739, 762, 763, 764, 920,
921, 922, 969-973
Safford, Philip
940
Saint Jerome
122
Salem, Greta
883
Salmon, Lucy M.
390
Salner, Marcia
715
Sandler, Bernice R.
705, 716
Savin, Marion B.
558
Schau, Candace Garrett
765
Schiebinger, Londa
030
Schilb, John
884
Schmitz, Betty
816, 862, 885, 886

INDEX B

SUBJECT
(Numbers in index indicate entry number.)

Kraków
  071

Language
  077
Larcom, Lucy
  387
Latin language
  089
Latinas
  849
Learned women
  027, 073, 074, 085, 095,
  106, 214, 568-574, 632
Liberal education
  793, 866, 873
Librarians
  415, 416, 441
Library
  415, 416, 441
Litchfield Female Academy
  545, 563, 565, 566
Literacy
  096, 175, 176, 180, 184,
  188
Livy
  036
London
  054
Lyon, Mary
  547, 549

Male attitudes toward
  educating women
  020, 031, 102
Mann, Horace
  564, 648
Martineau, Harriet
  375
Marxism
  692

Massachusetts
  187, 195, 372, 587, 663
Meyer, Annie Nathan
  615
Mid-Atlantic states
  349, 523
Middle Ages
  054-072
Midwives
  409, 411
Mill girls
  312, 380, 386-388, 395
Minority women
  825, 828, 838, 842
Missionary women
  275, 364
Mitchell, Lucy Sprague
  531, 592
Moral education
  782-785, 802, 803
More, Hannah
  114, 117
Motherhood and education
  212, 216, 237, 239, 263,
  279, 286, 296, 325, 382,
  474, 603, 780, 832
Mott, Lucretia
  461
Mount Holyoke College
  599
Mount Holyoke Seminary
  544, 557, 562, 599
Mulcaster, Richard
  115
Multicultural education
  812, 820

National Association of Colored
  Women's Clubs
  508
National Council for Research
  on Women
  695

Racism
843, 879
Radicalism
468
Reform movements (See also,
Progressive women)
485, 486, 488, 491
Reform periodicals
497
Reform school
242, 243
Reformation
093-100
Religion, influence on
education of women
008, 044, 048, 059, 060,
061, 062, 064, 065, 068,
088, 097, 098, 099, 100,
141, 177, 179, 181, 182,
183, 189, 190, 199, 217,
247, 249, 257, 260, 270,
274, 275, 803
Renaissance education
008, 073, 074, 076-080,
082, 084-089, 091, 092
Renaissance women
008, 063, 070, 073-092,
126
Republican mother
202-229
Research methods
004, 005, 007, 009, 012-
015, 016, 018
Resistance to change in
students
855
Roman women
035, 036, 038, 040, 041,
045-048, 053
Rousseau
023

Saint-Cyr, Marquis Laurent
104
Salonières
101, 105, 109
Salter, Thomas
079
Sappho
044
Schoolmarm
343, 346, 370
Schools
022, 066, 096, 166, 172,
177, 194, 197, 201, 207,
226, 227, 234, 243, 319,
324, 336, 343, 344, 346,
356, 360, 361, 362, 365,
367, 369, 370, 392, 454,
460, 537, 550, 555, 556,
565, 566, 576, 582, 583,
584, 585, 586, 587, 631,
718, 720, 722, 730, 733-
736, 746, 752, 756, 758,
759, 761-764, 774, 776,
828, 832, 833, 837, 841,
846, 847, 851, 863, 897,
907, 912, 920, 922, 930,
935, 937, 938, 949, 951,
963, 974, 975, 979, 983
Secondary education of women
033, 454, 460, 575-590,
847, 851
Seneca
047
Sentimental women
241, 244, 256, 260
Sex (see Gender)
Sex bias
875, 877, 910, 938
Sex equity in the classroom
901-928
Sex role socialization
743, 752, 753, 765, 775,
833, 858, 867, 907